Unraveling My Father's Suicide

Unraveling My Father's Suicide

KATHLEEN LAPLANTE

Editing by Stephen Parolini
Copyediting by Lora Schrock
Cover design by Samantha Malinay
Interior design and typesetting by Pat Reinheimer

ISBN 978-0-692-40988-6

9 8 7 6 5 4 3 2 1

With love
To my two sons
Kegan and Alden

Contents

Preface

The movie *Vantage Point* (2008) opens with an assassination attempt on the president of the United States of America. The remainder of the movie is taken up with five replays of that same attempt. Each replay is from the unique vantage point of one of the five main characters. Since all five were in different locations at the time of the attempt, and each had his or her own personal history with the president, the portrayals were markedly different. Yet they were all true in the context of the story.

So it would be with the story of my father's suicide. If my mother and my five brothers and sisters told their personal stories, those stories would be markedly different from each other, and from mine. Our seven vantage points would vary according to our age, gender, experiences, and the amount and quality of time we each spent with my father. Yet they would all be true in the context of his suicide.

My vantage point is the only one that has been captured in writing, but it has not been captured in isolation. My mother, most of my brothers and sisters, three of my aunts, and two of my cousins have all helped by verifying the facts, memories, and conversations that make up this memoir. If any inaccuracies exist, however, I take full responsibility for them.

Introduction

I entered the world on a cold winter day, January 24, 1962. It was 7:56 a.m. and I was in the Notre Dame Hospital in Manchester, New Hampshire. I don't remember any of my stay, but I know Mary was watching over me. She was the mother of Jesus, and the hospital was named after her. (Notre Dame is French for Our Lady, an endearing title Catholics use to refer to her.)

When my mother sufficiently recovered after my birth, she took me home to where my four older siblings greeted me. We became a family of seven, sort of: one boy, four girls, my mother, and my father, except he wasn't around a lot because he was out drinking so much. At that time, we were living in the South Elm Federal Housing Project.

Soon after my birth, my uncle Fred, who lived in California and was my father's brother, offered my father a job there. My mother took time to consider the idea and decided it would be beneficial. She thought it would get my father away from his drinking buddies and put him in a situation where he would cut back on booze altogether. So she agreed to go and we all moved.

My younger brother, Greg, was born there within the first year and we became a family of eight. We were three thousand miles from home and didn't know anyone except Uncle Fred. The situation quickly became grim because my father found new drinking buddies and continued to drink as much as he did before. My mother did not wait long to take action. She accepted money wired from my father's mother and bought airplane tickets to fly us all back to Manchester—without my father. She got rid of all our furniture when he was at work and then brought us to the airport.

Upon arrival in New Hampshire, we moved in with my maternal grandmother and step-grandfather for what turned out to be six weeks. We were three adults and six young children all squeezed into a small, two-bedroom, pink-aluminum-sided house. At night, my mother and grandparents rolled out some cots for us to sleep on, and they readied the couch as a makeshift bed for my mom. One of us also slept with my grandmother and one of us slept with my grandfather. I am not sure why they had separate bedrooms, but we made do and were grateful for the arrangements.

We eventually moved into the Rock Rimmon Federal Housing Project on the west side of Manchester, where my mother took my father back into our home. He had returned from California and that was the infancy stage of their get-out/no-come-back dynamic. It lasted many years. My father would do things like gamble with money they could not afford to waste, spend his paycheck on booze before he even got home from work, and cheat on my mother. It didn't matter. My mother would kick him out and always take him back.

My initial memories came from our time at Rock Rimmon Project. We moved there when I was about three years old. My mother, my father sometimes, and my five brothers and sisters and I lived in one of twelve apartments in our oblong brick building, of which there were a total of seventeen in the entire complex. That made up approximately two hundred families altogether. At the time, I didn't know it was a federal housing project for low-income families. I didn't even know what "low income" was. I just knew we had lots of kids to play with and lots of wonderful neighbors. One of them would go clam digging a few times a year and share her bounty with us and ask nothing in return. She was a fabulous role model of generosity for me, and I loved the instruction she gave on how to shuck the clams, dip them in heated broth and then in melted butter before popping the delicacy into our mouths.

We had woods nearby where we went blueberry picking. I often ate some of them while I was chewing pink bubblegum. I got such joy out of its transformation to purple bubblegum, because it seemed magical. The woods led down to Sandy Beach on the Piscataqua River, where we had many family outings and went swimming. Behind our building was the Bulletin, an undeveloped area of sand dunes and forest where we escaped to build forts and ride around on dirt bikes. In front of our building was a large grassy area with monkey bars, a merry-go-round, a slide, and more playground equipment. The dirt in the area became our palette for mixed media "drawing." We used pine needles to form houses with all kinds of rooms. And we used sticks to play Hangman, scratching out the framework for the body and the lines for the missing letters. We felt safe in our neighborhood.

My brothers and sisters and I attended St. Jean de Baptiste Catholic Elementary School. At seven years old, I received my First Communion in the associated St. Jean de Baptiste Church. I remember walking the mile to get to the complex. I also remember piling into a station wagon along with my siblings and some neighborhood children so my mother could drive us there during a snowfall. She must have borrowed the car from one of our neighbors because we didn't have one. Those were the days before mandatory seat belts, so we piled in and sat on each other's laps. God bless my mother for her patience in handling all of us.

Most of the city's French Canadian immigrants lived on the

west side, although some had migrated to the east side as well. The many Catholic churches on both sides of the city reflected this ethnic influence: St. Jean de Baptiste, St. Marie, St. Anne, St. Joseph, and St. Augustine, among others. The Polish, the Irish, and the Italians maintained their own Catholic churches back then. The different ethnic groups didn't blend until the 1980s, when boundaries were dissolving and the flow of parishioners was becoming more fluid throughout the city. I imagine language barriers were dissipating, too.

When I was eight years old, we moved across town to the Corey Square neighborhood on the east side of Manchester. Our family settled in federal housing again, but it was much different than the multi-unit project on the west side. On the west side, the project was set aside from all other residences in the area. It was constructed on a one hundred fifty-acre swath of land with seventeen long buildings each containing twelve apartments. The approximate two hundred families were essentially self-contained within their own large neighborhood, and if a friend came to visit, they knew it was the poor part of town.

On the east side, our neighborhood had only two federal apartment buildings, one perpendicular to the other. Our building housed only three families and the other building housed several elderly people. I remember when we first stepped into our new home. Since we never had an upstairs before, I was so thrilled to see a stairway to a second floor. The bedrooms and the larger bathroom were up there. That bathroom had a shower and we were ecstatic, because on the west side, we only had a bathtub. In addition to those amenities, we had another half bath downstairs.

Instead of an all-brick exterior, the lower level of our building was constructed with brick, while the upper level was constructed with white siding. The design helped us blend in with the rest of the neighborhood, and if friends came to visit, they did not necessarily know they were in with poor families.

We walked to the public elementary school a few blocks away. Patrol leaders guided children by foot to their homes after school. Besides learning history, science, music, and math, we learned safety for crossing the streets, safety for riding bicycles, and proper techniques for brushing our teeth. My oldest sister, Diane, and my brother, Don, had a longer walk since they attended the junior high school.

There were no woods next to our house, but parks were just a fifteen-minute walk away. We played tennis and Little League baseball there, and we climbed playground equipment. Sometimes we just enjoyed each other's company. During off-hours, the elementary school's tar-paved yard became our stomping ground where we played kickball, hopscotch, jump rope, basketball, and delinquency. Delinquency wasn't a game. It was the trouble my siblings and I got into. We broke into the school building more than once and we visited various rooms. We stole ice cream bars and rushed out hoping we wouldn't get caught. I always wondered if we would have been more upright as teenagers if we stayed in the Catholic school on the west side.

The Merrimack River divided the east and west sides of our city. Several colossal red brick buildings lined the river and made up what was known as the Mill Buildings. Weaving, electric sheet-metal working, sweater making, rifle making, and soup canning were some of the jobs performed there by adults and children. Thankfully, child labor had stopped before I was born.

Manchester was nicknamed the Queen City because it had the largest population in the state of New Hampshire without being its capital city. Civic organizations held several parades throughout the year. I marched in one Christmas parade with a colorfully wrapped box around my upper body; I was a Christmas gift to the city! And then there was the Memorial Day parade when I rode on a float with my gymnastics team. Along with the Fourth of July and St. Patrick's Day parades, these events brought residents together like no other activity. We took pleasure in them on the downtown strip on the east side. That strip was where we went shopping and shoplifting, dining out, and working high school jobs.

My mother worked on that strip as well. She finished freshly made donuts, filling them with creams and jellies and covering them with glazes and jimmies. I was hired in the same restaurant as a waitress. I enjoyed the fast pace during busy times, the option to make more money by working at other stores on weekends, the generally pleasant staff, and even the grubby little men who came in from the back alley to eat the day's leftover donuts.

On the east side, we attended the public elementary, junior high, and high schools. The north end was where the wealthier residents lived, but their children attended the same junior high and high schools as us poorer students. Mingling with them gave me the feeling that I had stepped up in the world. When I got braces in eighth grade, I felt "cool" because I was just like the rich kids who had them. I never told any of them that federal and state government programs had paid for mine.

In high school, I was salutatorian of my high school class. During that time, I was a gymnast, a cheerleader, a summer attendee at a private prep school, an employee at the local donut shop, an orator, and a poetry reader. My father was hardly around, while my mother always attended my events. I was a typical teenager in that I was self-absorbed and not as grateful as I should have been for all that my mother did for me.

I applied to several colleges and decided to go to the University of New Hampshire (UNH) where I was given just about a full scholarship. That certainly helped my financial situation as well as my emotional one. I was not ready to move far away from home; in fact, my mother came through for me most of my freshman year. Almost every Friday afternoon, she drove to UNH to bring me home, and every Sunday afternoon, she drove me back to school. Part of my impetus was having a boyfriend back home, and part of it was the social pressure I felt from living in the dormitories. I was so glad to have an outlet from what seemed to be a strange living arrangement.

1

Into the Abyss

I woke up in a haze one morning in the middle of my junior year at college. It was January 25, 1983, the day after my twenty-first birthday. I could barely make out the silhouettes of the two people standing in front of my bed. They were saying something, but their words were unclear, not because they were mumbling, but because my hearing hadn't yet caught up with my seeing. When I realized these two people were my sisters, Diane and Patty, I groggily asked, "What are you doing? It's so early." I couldn't make sense of what was happening. My sisters had never come to visit me at college, never mind at 6:30 in the morning.

The fact that I was hung over didn't help. I had gone out drinking the night before with my friends to commemorate my coming of legal age. We had gone barhopping and enjoyed more than our share of alcoholic drinks. Not surprisingly, my head was pulsing that next morning.

I couldn't think about any plans I may have made for the day, never mind what the weather was like. Once my hearing kicked in, though, I clearly heard Diane and Patty tell me my father committed suicide yesterday. They said he did it in his apartment back in Manchester, the city where we grew up. "What do you mean Dad committed suicide yesterday? That was my birthday," I muttered. The horror of such news threw my equilibrium off, and the fact that I hadn't seen my father for years augmented my confusion. He was an active alcoholic who pranced in and out of my life from the day I was born, and when he pranced in, he was usually drunk and often hurting my mother. I had no contact with him since I started college, and I rarely thought about him. But this current news demanded my attention.

"We're here to give you a ride home," my sisters continued.

"A ride home?" The meaning of those words didn't register. *"Why would I go home?"* I wondered. *"What would I do there?"*

My feelings hadn't kicked in for the day, so I had no way of knowing if I needed support from my mom or my brothers and sisters. Then again, even if my feelings were functioning, I don't think they would have prompted me to go home. I came from an emotionally disconnected family, and I felt little sense of comfort within it. I didn't confide in my mother or siblings about my inner world, and they didn't confide in me about theirs. So, *Why would I go home?* was a reasonable question. The thought never came to me to go home and comfort anyone else instead.

Two other factors complicated the situation in front of me. One was my feeling physically disoriented. I had recently moved to college for the last half of my junior year. Out of nowhere, I would have to reverse it all and move back home with all of my brothers and sisters. It would only be a temporary change, but it was one I felt incapable of making. So I did the only thing I knew and that was to stay at school.

The second confounding factor was my lack of context. I had little sense of what happens in a family's life when someone dies, so my sense of obligation was minimal to the situation at hand. The only exposure I had to funerals was a framed photograph of my grandmother's sister, Matante Rosa, in an open casket. I was twelve years old when she passed away. My grandmother kept her photo on her dresser and I looked at it when I played hide-and-seek in her bedroom. I remember thinking my great aunt looked so pretty in her lovely blue dress. She also looked peaceful as she lay on the pillowy, ivory-colored silk lining of her casket.

Everything was happening so quickly. My sisters' alarming news, which was overwhelming in itself, was complicated by the fact that I hardly knew my father. *"What am I supposed to think? How am I supposed to feel? Who is this man? This is insane."*

I couldn't access any significant emotional connection to him, not even at the shocking news of his death. I simply didn't know him, especially during the latter part of high school and all of college. He spent so much time at the bars, and such fleeting time at home, we were never able to develop any depth to our relationship. I did develop, however, a pit inside my stomach. It was longing to be filled with memories, time, and knowledge of him.

The minimal connection I did have with him was laden with embarrassment, shame, and confusion, all of which further impeded my thinking. I couldn't find a single reason to go home. When my sisters and I talked about it, to their surprise, I made a final decision to stay at school. I had classes to attend and I was too stymied to do anything else. Diane and Patty drove home without me.

At school, my friends and professors gave me personal condolences and sympathy cards. Their gestures were quite moving and became catalysts for awakening me to the complex nature of my situation. A day or so later, an emotional upheaval finally registered. I broke down in tears between classes and realized I had to go home. I couldn't be alone to face the reality of my father re-entering my life, never mind that he did so by hanging himself with a belt.

Having made my decision, I went to my professor's office to tell him I would be missing class. I was taken aback when he asked me how my father "did it." Tears welled in my eyes. It was my first realization that many people do not know how insular and private suicide usually is. They have never learned about the particular shame and grief those left behind after a suicide have to face.

I desperately wanted to leave my professor's office, but I couldn't find the words or the strength to escape what had become an uncomfortable situation, made more invasive by the cramped nature of the room. So I answered his question. I shared the details of my father's self-murder. Looking back, I came to believe that my professor wasn't acting with malintent. He had a good heart and was generally kind. I believe he had been acting from ignorance.

The wake was surreal. My brother Greg wasn't there. He had moved to California four years earlier and decided not to come home for my father's services. So I stood with my older brother, Don, and my mother and sisters in the receiving line next to my father's casket.

I wanted to scream. Dissonance pulsed through my body. *"Why am I standing in this line? Why is his girlfriend in the shadows? She's been with him for more than ten years. She should be here, not us, not this **impostor** of a family. And who is that man in the casket? He's not my father. My father was tall."* I remembered him in photos, handsome and lean.

In the casket, he looked pudgy and short, even shorter than I was. And his hands were fat, too big for his body. I had to work hard to maintain composure in the face of these unexpected findings, so I compartmentalized them along with the unresolved emotions I had stashed away since the chilling wake-up call from my sisters.

The next day, we had the funeral service. None of us knew what to say or how to say it. I wasn't very religious at the time, so the ceremony didn't resonate with me. I don't recall much of it. I do remember feeling uneasy about my father being cremated and left to "rest" in a crypt. *How can we say we buried him if we leave him in an urn behind a granite wall for eternity?* I wondered. This was another unexpected enigma for my brain to process. I knew I wanted to be buried in the ground without a casket or burial vault. I wanted my flesh and bones to decay naturally back into the soil. So cremation didn't fit my definition of "burying" my dad.

But I wasn't involved in the decision-making, and that was probably a good thing. I had a tendency to be abrasive in family discussions. My mother and Patty handled the arrangements, and despite my predisposition about cremation, I think they did a tremendous job.

I don't remember how many days we all stayed home; I think it was less than a week. I imagine my siblings and my mother experienced some dissociation similar to mine, but I don't know. We didn't talk about my father's suicide or about our internal experiences. It was as if we had all come home for a visit, talked about everything except our dad, and then vanished back to our former lives. I left when I felt the need to return to my everyday life, as if a college student with an absent, alcoholic father who committed suicide could do such a thing.

Memorable Minutiae One

When I was discouraged by remembering so many upsetting memories of my father, balance came forth and I began to recall intimate moments when he touched my heart. Those good memories are first on these pages. Sad and painful memories are second. In one instance, a memory is both good and bad.

My father carried me up the hill from Sandy Beach one time to give me medical attention after I fell on a piece of glass. My left knee was bleeding and he patched it up. In that moment, he became a hero in my eyes. I still have the scar.

One night, my father came home drunk to our apartment in the Rock Rimmon Federal Housing Project. He started abusively hitting my mother, so she called out to neighbors for help. When one arrived, my mother called the police. My father attempted to escape by running out the back door, and in doing so, he hit his head on one of the metal clothes line poles in our backyard. At least that's what the police told my mother. She didn't believe their story. She thought they had beat up my father while attempting to capture him. Nonetheless, they arrested him. Later that week my mother went with our neighbor to file a criminal complaint. Nothing came of it.

2

After the Funeral

It was many months, maybe years, before my siblings and I talked about the suicide. When we did, we only talked concrete details. "Was there any food in Dad's refrigerator? How much beer was there? Beer and condiments? That's all? What happened to his belt? Did Uncle Édouard know the name of the police officer who called him to identify Dad? Who was it that went to the apartment afterward?"

We didn't talk emotions. We didn't talk about how we felt or how our lives had been impacted by this violent act. Hence, I don't know what my mother and siblings were thinking or feeling. Neither do I know what I was thinking or feeling most of the time. We all seemed to be emotionally numb, in a gaping hole, quite likely a reflection of all of us being in denial about the horrific impact of my father's suicide. Our numbness was probably not just a direct result of the suicide, but also the lingering effect of the family-wide oppression established in our alcoholic household years ago. Both dynamics stunted my family such that we rarely engaged in heartfelt and constructive dialogue.

Little did we know that the impact of my father's suicide would be far-reaching to our yet-to-be-born-children and grandchildren. After all, a hole is left in one's soul even having a distant grandfather or great-grandfather who suicided. At least that's my belief, and I believe it's also true for survivors who don't even know they have suicide in their family lineage.

When I returned to school after the funeral, I struggled to resume my everyday life because I had lost my rhythm of normalcy. Self-defeating behaviors didn't help, although it felt like they were helping at the time. I was eating a lot less food, running longer distances than before, and exercising a great deal more. Every day I had the same menu. I had a cup of coffee in the morning, and at lunch, I ate half a pita pocket sandwich with a thin slice of turkey and lettuce. That was it. I was already thin for my height, but I lost quite a bit more weight during that uncertain season.

People expressed concern about my size two appearance, but I downplayed their worry and enjoyed the attention. I also liked the mini high I experienced from feeling like I had control over my body. It was fueled by a false sense of empowerment, which led me to believe I had control over *all* of my life.

During that time, I masked my inner world with outer-world accomplishments. I kept up with homework, I went out with friends, and I received A's in all my courses, eventually graduating number one in my class of chemical engineers. My academic record proved to be instrumental in getting me out from under the dark cloud hovering over me. It helped me obtain quality summer internships and post-graduation jobs with large corporations like Johnson & Johnson and IBM.

During my last year and a half in college, I continued to drink excessively, often culminating in blackouts. My friends found it amusing and challenged me to drinking contests, which I usually won. After I graduated and started working, I cut back on my drinking, but my challenges with food continued well into my adult life. It wasn't until I started grasping the psychology and spirituality of life—of my life in particular—that I developed a yearning to eat more food. I finally began to feel like I deserved good things, even if it was on an unconscious level.

Inwardly, my life was crippled. I didn't enjoy time with my boyfriend or my girl friends. I couldn't bring myself to open up to anyone about my feelings and thoughts. I felt empty, secretly longing for intimacy but unable to achieve it. I had no idea that the imbalance I was creating with my studying, diet, exercise, and social life was contributing to the emotional imbalance I was experiencing. At times, I struggled to feel anything about my father's death. At other times, I was laden with grief, but I couldn't discern what I was grieving. Was it that I no longer had a father? Or was it that I never had one to begin with? Maybe I was grieving about having had a father who was such a disgrace, or maybe my lament was about losing all possibility of ever enjoying a tender moment with him. Most likely, I was grieving all those things at the same time. The intensity was frightening, and I thought something was wrong with me.

In retrospect, I realize I was completely normal. I was merely experiencing multiple feelings at the same time. It's called ambivalence, a word I hadn't yet learned. When I did learn it, my feelings gushed forth. I had a hard time slowing down to identify and properly work through the anger and self-hatred I had harbored for so many years, that they became repressed again.

Most people had no idea of the pain I was in. It was the kind of pain that leads a person to believe no one likes them, the kind of pain that leads a person to believe they have nothing to offer the rest of the world, and the kind of pain that leads a person to experience excruciating loneliness, even when among friends. It was also the kind of pain that ferments in the deep hollows of one's soul, to later manifest by leading that person to contemplate suicide.

A year after I graduated from college, I married a classmate. I essentially stopped drinking due to lack of interest, but my challenges with food continued. Four years into our marriage, we had our first son, Kegan, and sixteen months later we had our second son, Alden. I had vivid and violent dreams with each pregnancy. In them, I was chased and raped. I was violated. I believe it was a reflection of how I felt in my subconscious. Given my struggles with body image and the trauma I experienced growing up in an alcoholic and dysfunctional environment, my interpretation seemed sensible. After all, my body *was* being invaded—by my very own babies.

The nightmares made me sad and uneasy. I had exerted so much effort to control my eating and my body, only to end up with no control whatsoever. I felt burdened by the very children I consciously created with my husband. The irony was painful and baffling.

Motherhood was difficult for me, partially because I had little experience taking care of children while I was growing up. I never felt comfortable around them. I didn't know how to discipline them and I was certain they didn't like me, just like our cat didn't like me. While babysitting the children next door, I spent most of the time fighting with the eight year old. I couldn't wait until their mother came home. I simply did not know how to relax and be playful. I was scared.

I was more playful with my own children, but I still felt out of sorts. I was out of balance in the other areas of my life, where I stretched myself thin trying to "do it all" as engineer, wife, mother, neighbor, house cleaner, and so much more. A sense of being overwhelmed took its toll on my emotions and I eventually made an appointment with a counselor, Brad, in the Employee Assistance Program (EAP) at my company. He didn't hesitate to suggest I make an appointment with a professional psychotherapist, and I didn't hesitate to tell him I wanted nothing to do with that recommendation, primarily because the only thing I knew about psychotherapy was what I saw on *The Bob Newhart Show*. It petrified me. But in the end, Brad talked me through my fears and reassured me. I took his suggestion and made an appointment, primarily because I was in too much pain not to.

The first therapist I met with was William. He was kind but not outgoing enough. I knew he wasn't a good fit for me, so I didn't make a future appointment. A week passed and Brad called me to see how things went. I relayed my experience to him, and he suggested I call William back and ask him for a referral. Brad did everything he could to make this easy for me. He even told me how to word my request: "Do you know of another therapist who is more active in his treatment approach?"

The idea of calling William back both startled and frightened me. I was sure the man would get angry with me, and I couldn't foresee being able to handle his ire. I was virtually handcuffed by my fear of confrontation.

I eventually faced that fear and called William. I was pleasantly surprised when he was understanding and readily recommended one of his colleagues. He wasn't angry at all. With pure grit, I made an appointment with the second counselor, Dr. Markem. I ended up working with him for eleven years, which gave me reason to believe our coming together was divinely inspired. Through our work, the mystery and science of therapy unfolded. A successful medical treatment emerged for me, and so did an instrument for me to unravel the mysteries of life, of my life in particular.

Looking back, I am thankful that Brad called to follow up on my first appointment. If he hadn't, there's a good chance I would have abandoned psychotherapy altogether or I would have had a rough journey back. I certainly had no intentions to continue after I saw William. Brad ended up being an angel in my life. He led me to a therapist who was a wonderful fit for me. Dr. Markem was the first person with whom I discussed my father and his suicide. He was also the person who helped me understand that self-defeating behaviors were common after such a traumatic event. That knowledge provided me with a sense of relief, because it was the rhyme and reason for my unending angst. Once I knew the origin of the problem, I could finally begin to construct a coping strategy and solution to overcome it.

After Dr. Markem took my personal history, he determined that I probably had dysthymia—a low-grade form of depression— during my younger years. Dysthymia is chronic, but its symptoms are less severe than those associated with major depression. A person's moods are consistently low enough to be debilitating at times but not paralyzing.

My moods were low and irritable, and I was never satisfied with the significant accomplishments I achieved. The list wasn't small: an A-student, a gymnast who competed around the state, a cheerleader, a winner of multiple speech contests, a salutatorian, a college scholarship winner, a third place winner in a poetry reading contest, a dedicated worker at a local eatery, a winner of math and French language prizes, and more. Thanks to therapy, I was gradually able to squelch my reticence and appreciate my achievements, but it took a lot of time.

Social settings proved to be a challenge for me as well. I never felt like I could be myself in a crowd, in one-on-one situations, or even alone. While those feelings are common among teenagers and young adults, for me, they led to destructive behaviors, like drinking excessively. It was easier for me to relax and feel connected with people after I had some beer or wine. Peers saw me as someone who was having fun and was happy with her achievements, but on the inside, I was aching to feel loved and yearning to know how to love others.

My second son, Alden, was born during my initial year of therapy. Kegan was sixteen months old and postpartum depression came down upon me. When that didn't subside, it became clear I was dealing with major depression, an illness about which I knew very little. I didn't even know it was considered an illness, never mind a potentially chronic one. Then again, if I had been told it could become chronic, I might not have understood its severity. I had no previous exposure to anyone contending with long-term health challenges. This segue into the world of mental health, where I struggled to understand and live with a serious illness, was more than an unwanted arrival; it was a harrowing upheaval.

After going to therapy a while longer, I still couldn't reach sufficient clarity about what I was supposed to do in all my roles, or what I *wanted* to do in all of them. I felt trapped in the dark with no ray of light breaking through. That led to incessant thoughts of suicide, so my therapist suggested I see a psychiatrist for medication.

"Medication? Are you crazy? I am *not* taking drugs." That was my reaction. I rarely took aspirin and I wasn't about to start taking more serious drugs. Drugs. That's how I thought of all medication. I held them on the same level as cocaine and heroin. I even asked, "How is my taking these drugs any different from my father using alcohol?" I argued with my therapist about it for nearly an entire year.

After I became desperate from struggling to take care of my children, to maintain my performance at work, and to keep some semblance of a marriage with my husband, I relented and saw a psychiatrist. He started me on Prozac at what was considered to be the therapeutic dose. Very soon after starting it, my thoughts began to race with no reprieve, and my body felt like it was going to explode. I was constantly restless and wasn't able to sleep. Suicide came to the forefront of my thinking once again. This time it was obsessive. As sometimes happens, the medicine was actually causing me to be more suicidal than I was without it.

My therapist was the first person to suggest that I might need to go to the hospital, but I resisted his idea again. "Hospital? What do you mean, a mental hospital? No way. We used to make fun of places like that when I was growing up. That's a place for nutties," I pushed back. I wasn't in control. My reactions soon heightened, and I had no choice but to admit myself into the hospital.

As the nursing staff checked me in, I watched a patient obtain her nighttime medications. She said rather loudly, "Oh, good, the pink one's there." I was convinced the place was a house for crazies and I shut down. The admitting nurse sensed my closed-mindedness and feeling of entrapment. She told me to give the other patients a chance. I rolled my eyes, but with time, I befriended them, even the one who was thankful for the pink pill. As it turned out, she was just joking. But I had no idea at the time.

Later on, I realized I had been contributing to the terrible misunderstanding so many people have about mental health. Like them, I was highly judgmental of others. I kept the hospital patients at a distance by holding onto the belief that I was better than they were. *"Sure, they're fun and straightforward people, but they're also on the loony edge, so there is no way I'm getting close to them."* But just by being their natural selves, my fellow inpatients soon enlightened me about nonjudgmental acceptance. They included me in everything, even when I closed myself off to them, and that was humbling and eye opening. I learned more about mental health, acceptance, and love in that hospital than I had learned anywhere else until that time.

The doctor quickly assessed my medications and took me off Prozac. I was clearly sensitive to its side effects, so he switched me to a medication with more history, a tricyclic antidepressant called nortriptyline. It was introduced and used in the medical field earlier, so there was more data available at the time. Since I was able to tolerate the dry mouth, constipation, and dizziness that accompanied it, my body was able to reach an effective dose of the antidepressant, such that my emotions became more manageable.

Years later, nortriptyline was no longer effective for me and my depression became severe again. I had to try other medications. Knowing the dangers of using them without supervision, I worked with a female psychiatrist, Dr. Phillips, to manage the maze of psychopharmacological medicines. She served me well, especially when I opted to try Prozac a second time. Dr. Phillips was like a coach. She helped me tolerate the associated mental and physical discomforts at various dosage levels, and she introduced the addition of other carefully selected compounds, like a low dose of lithium carbonate. She recommended this to augment the effectiveness of the Prozac.

When I later decided to discontinue my medications under the supervision of Dr. Phillips, I eventually experienced a depressive crash after a hypomanic episode. Hypomania (bipolar II) is a lower manifestation of what is more commonly known as mania (bipolar I), the state people are in when they go shopping and buy thousands of dollars of clothes or they gamble and lose the equivalent amount, often when they cannot afford to do such things. Their behavior is on the destructive side and their illness is easy to detect. With hypomania, however, a person tends to appear less destructive. They present themselves as extra productive with success and are therefore embraced and often lauded by others. Their illness is more difficult to detect.

For me, previously having lithium in my medication regime as an augmenter for my antidepressant proved to be advantageous when it was discovered that I was bipolar II. That is because lithium is commonly used to treat bipolar I and II. The combination has worked well for me for over twelve years, and while my depression and hypomania have not completely disappeared, they are less debilitating.

Memorable Minutiae Two

My father was an accomplished pocket billiard player in Manchester's Queen City Pool League and its Hall of Fame.

When my father was a young child, my grandparents placed him in a local orphanage. He slept there overnight for several months while his seven brothers and sisters remained at home. The purpose seems to have been some sort of childcare, but no one is certain. What is certain is that he went home every weekend, and when it was time for him to return to the orphanage on Sunday, my father and his siblings were sad to say goodbye.

3

Return to the Mausoleum

One Saturday morning when Kegan was two, I put him in his car seat in the back of our old, boxy Volvo station wagon. It was a flat, mint-green color, and because it was used, its exterior was dotted with rust. We were going to run errands. As we headed to our third stop, thoughts about my father arose out of the blue. *I wonder if anyone's gone to visit him at the mausoleum. It's been so long. I can't believe I've never gone back.*

My eyes welled up and I took a deep breath. I became consumed by my emotions and pulled over on the side of the road to collect myself, but instead I broke down into nonstop, forceful sobs. I was so sad for my father and all the family bonding he missed out on. I was also sad for my own losses associated with the different roles he should have played in my life: loving parent, guardian, protector, father, disciplinarian, mentor.

As I sobbed, I realized I was releasing the tension of a secret I had carried for years. I never told anyone, but I was actually glad my father died, or at least a significant part of me was. I remember thinking, *"Oh, my gosh, I don't ever have to worry again about being with my friends and running into him when he's drunk. Thank God."*

There was no way I would admit that to anyone, not even my brothers and sisters, not even many years later. I was convinced none of them would understand and thought they would think exactly what I was thinking at that time—that I was being unjustifiably selfish.

Tears continued to pour forth as feelings of guilt arose. *"How can I be glad my own father died?"* I sobbed, but I eventually allowed myself to own my feelings. *"It is what it is,"* I thought. *"I'm glad he's gone."* It was such a relief to openly acknowledge that truth to myself. Unfortunately, or maybe fortunately, feelings of shame and guilt washed over me again. I was confused and liberated at the same time.

I felt compelled to go to my father's cemetery site. "I need to talk to you 'in person,'" I said to him from the side of the road. "And I want you to meet your grandson." I calmed down and drove home, where I presented my broken self to my husband. I asked him to watch our younger son, so I could take our older one with me to the mausoleum. Thankfully, he said yes.

I drove to the cemetery and went straight to the mausoleum where my father's ashes are kept in a crypt. I was looking forward to paying my respects, but I really wished I was paying respect to a father I deeply admired. Once I reached the section where he is kept, I held my son up to him. Tears streamed down my face as I struggled to get words out. I didn't care if anyone else noticed. I was blubbering and mumbling, "See, this is what you missed out on. You have a grandson and you're not even here to get to know him. You'll never get to know him and that makes me so sad."

It was strange talking to him, especially since we barely talked when he was alive. Memories of him lapsed and my feelings about our relationship were somewhat frozen. I was at a loss of what to say, and then suddenly, I remembered an incident with him. I was thirteen years old and he called our house. He was drunk.

In the teasing tone of a high school boy annoying his sister, my father asked me, "Have you smoked pot yet?" I thought for sure an immature, "Na na naa na naa na" would follow, but his drunken drivel went to another topic. I was too dumbfounded to admonish him. Instead, I rolled my eyes and motioned to my brother Don to take the phone. He started walking over, but in my frustration and anger toward my father, I hurled the receiver at Don's abdomen. He had to fumble to catch it. "There is no way I'm staying on the phone with that jerk," I grumbled.

When the disturbing memory dissipated, I stood dazed in front of my father's crypt. There I was trying to get close to him, and at the same time, I was feeling relieved because I'd never have to talk to him again. I didn't have enough time to resolve these seemingly contradictory reactions because the mausoleum was closing for the day. I didn't know it closed on a daily basis, but I felt fortunate for having the hour I had at that intense time in my life. I picked up my son, walked to my car, and drove home.

It wasn't until several years later that I began to understand the religious significance of the grounds at my father's cemetery. It's not that I didn't notice things like a crucified Christ hanging on the cross in the chapel, or the statue of Mary holding Jesus right after He was taken off the cross; I just didn't understand their relevance. And I had been raised Catholic.

My catechesis as a child had been subpar. My mother, stretched thin from raising six children, often insisted that we go to Mass while she stayed home. I think it was a way for her to get time to herself. Without her as our chaperone or role model, though, we ended up consistently disobeying her.

We would head to church as expected, but once we were there, we'd skip Mass. We'd go across the street to the church-owned building and bowl in the downstairs bowling alley. Then we would slip back into the church hall to eat donuts before the rest of the congregation arrived. We concluded our deception by bringing home a copy of the weekly church bulletin. It served as "evidence" that we had gone to Mass.

This total disregard for my mother continued until I was fourteen years old. At that age, I received the sacrament of Confirmation, which is a type of initiation into adulthood. Religiously, I was supposed to be deepening my embrace of Jesus as my savior. It was also meant to be a time of becoming enriched and strengthened by the Holy Spirit, to protect and spread the faith. Instead, I abandoned it altogether. I stopped going to Mass, and I stopped educating myself on the deeper mysteries of my religion. The local church wasn't helpful because it didn't have any compelling programs for teenagers. That fueled my indifference and rejection, such that my young adult life disintegrated into a lifestyle of self-pride, arrogance, and misguided self-will.

I was therefore oblivious to the religious references and providence surrounding me at the mausoleum. I was also ignorant about the Catholic Church's teaching on suicide, although I did know in general, that the salvation of my father's soul could be in jeopardy.

It wasn't until fourteen years later that I learned more about it during a spiritual and religious conversion I had in 1997. I returned to the Catholic Church then, and many things became clear. For one, I was able to absorb the profundity of the cemetery's name. In the Bible, Mount Calvary was where Jesus hung and died on the cross before His Resurrection. This connection made me hopeful, if only for a moment, as I wondered if Mount Calvary Cemetery could be the place where my father might be resurrected.

When I asked my spiritual counselor about the Church's teaching on suicide, my heart sank. If my dad was completely culpable for taking his own life, his last act would be considered a mortal sin, and his soul would be cut off from God and His grace forever. That is, his soul would go to hell. The same would be true if God offered him mercy and for some reason he refused. Since we all have free will and can say, "No," at any time, that is a possibility.

I was distraught. "Is there any chance my father would have been spared that final judgment?" I asked. "What about his culpability? Do we know for sure that it was complete?"

My spiritual counselor explained that we cannot determine my father's culpability, and we don't know for sure if he is in heaven or in hell. God is the only one who knows that. Still, I was troubled, so I did some reading in the *Catechism of the Catholic Church*. Paragraph number 2282 says, "Grave psychological disturbances, anguish, or grave fear of hardship, suffering, or torture can diminish the responsibility of the one committing suicide." My father had two biologically based illnesses: untreated alcoholism and untreated depression. They are both known to impair one's thinking and intentions, so I felt another surge of hope. In my interpretation, his illnesses could have readily impeded his ability to make proper decisions at the time of his death, and that would mean he might not have been totally culpable for his act of suicide.

This finding was a light at the end of a dark tunnel. I still didn't know if my father was in heaven or hell, but at least I knew there was a possibility he was in heaven. That made it reasonable for me to act on my hope by praying for the salvation of his soul. The *Catechism of the Catholic Church* confirms this for my father and for all people who have taken their own lives. "2283 We should not despair of the eternal salvation of persons who have taken their own lives. By ways known to him alone, God can provide the opportunity for salutary repentance. The Church prays for persons who have taken their own lives."

In reflecting back, I now believe those prayers had to be a grace from God, because on the human level, I still resented my dad. I never would have started praying for him of my own accord.

Memorable Minutiae Three

When my father shaved, he put tiny pieces of toilet paper over the inevitable nicks and cuts. The small patches of blood seeping through intrigued me, and in a strange way, endeared him to me. When it came time for me to shave my legs for the first time, I shaved like he did and ended up with my fair share of nicks and cuts. I was glad to know the toilet paper trick.

My sister Lynn went to her friend Marta's house to hang out after school one day. When they arrived, Marta's mother wasn't home, but my father was there. Lynn was confused. There had been no previous connection between our two families. It wasn't until much later that she told my mother about the encounter. My mother suspected my father was cheating on her with this girl's mother, and she courageously confronted him one night. He claimed that Lynn was lying and he outright denied he was at that woman's house. That woman eventually became my father's steady and long-term girlfriend. She was the one at his funeral.

4

The Holy Catholic Bible

Members of my father's labor union came to pay their respects at the funeral. They were large men who loomed over the crowd, but they were also compassionate and kind. They gave my mother a wooden, aromatic cedar box, and inside the box was a white, leather-bound Bible in memory of my father.

It was a Catholic Bible, but since I wasn't a practicing Catholic at the time, or religious in any way, I took little interest in it. I knew my mother was holding on to it, and that was pretty much the extent of my connection with it that first year and a half after the funeral. Then, one day, I was sitting on my mother's living room floor reading the newspaper. She was putzing around, moving boxes, and tidying things up, when out of the blue, she told me she thought I should have the Bible.

I don't know if it was a spontaneous decision or if she'd been thinking about it for a while. Either way, I was quite touched by my mother's gesture. I was also surprised. We hadn't talked about my father's death for over a year. Her action was powerful because it was the first overt acknowledgment of the unorthodox bond cemented between my father and me, when he took his life on my birthday. It was a bond no other sibling could claim, not that they would want to, and it is one reason my healing process was unique in my family.

"It makes sense, don't you think?" my mother asked. I didn't know what to say. I was dumbfounded. I was also wondering if my brothers and sisters would be upset with her assessment.

It wasn't long afterward that I mentioned the exchange to one of my sisters. She became notably upset. "Why should you have the Bible?" she asked. "Maybe one of the rest of us would have wanted it. I don't think you should have necessarily gotten it by default."

I felt like someone had just stabbed me and I wanted to scream. *"Am I the only one who gets what happened? Why can't anyone see there's something different about my experience? Why can't they see the uncanny and eerie life and death connection between Dad and me? This Bible is probably the only good thing about his suicide, and they have to ruin it for me."*

In the end, I didn't let the complaint sway my decision to keep the Memorial Bible, even though I didn't know how to delve into it yet. I suspect I kept it because it was the only physical thing I had to hold to "feel" my father, to create an emotional and spiritual bond with him.

At some later point, I quieted myself and took time to look more carefully at the book. I ran my fingers across the white leather binding. It was supple and sturdy. Then I ran my fingers lightly over the shiny gold lettering on the cover, and I did the same with the shiny gold lettering on the spine. I opened the book to glossy pages that were cold to the touch, yet picturesque. Some had prayers for strength and guidance, and some had devout depictions of the Holy Catholic Mass. There were glossy pages in the back of the book, too, depicting scenes from Jesus' life and landscapes of the Holy Land.

The most surprising find was a recording section in the front. Therein lay catalogues for living ancestors to record the family history of the deceased. The pages included *In Loving Memory,*

Marriages, Births, Deaths, and Membership Record. The catalogues themselves were not that surprising, but the fact that my mother actually recorded our family information in them was. She wrote it all in the elegant cursive penmanship she had learned during her own Catholic education.

My thoughts multiplied when I saw it all. First, I considered it a loving gesture from my mother to my father, but then I was confused because I thought my mother didn't love him anymore. After all, she kicked him out of the house years ago. She packed his clothes and left them on the porch. She fought him for child support and won. Her seemingly conflicting actions confused me, and I was disappointed. *"How could Mom record all these things and not tell us? Not tell me?"* I felt as though she intentionally pushed me aside, and I couldn't understand her seemingly conflicting actions and mindset. Of course, she didn't owe it to me to share such details, but it would have been comforting.

The spaces on the *In Loving Memory* page—Dates and Places of Birth, Death, Interment of the Deceased —had been left blank. She filled in other pages though. On *Marriages*, she recorded the day of their Holy Matrimony in 1957. The page showed an illustration of a happy bride and groom who did not reflect my parents' life together. Neither did it seem to reflect their lives at the time of their actual wedding. I did the math. The wedding date was a little more than four months before Diane's birth. That was the first I learned of my parents' crisis pregnancy. I was in disbelief, and I experienced a latent concern for her and my father back then in their teenage years. I wanted to hug them and congratulate them. A baby, a new human being, was being entrusted to them and they embraced it at eighteen years old. They could have sought out an abortion or adoption, but they didn't.

Once again, though, I was disappointed with my mother. *Why didn't she tell me about this?* She didn't even mention it when I founded and headed up a walkathon for women and girls facing crisis pregnancies. And she was the head volunteer at the registration table each year. Of course, I was coming from a limited view of the world, but I felt that she owed me such details, until I realized later that some personal things simply do not get discussed during the passing of the baton from one generation to another. Besides, I had done a lot of work (and it is hard work) in therapy to release my parents as mental hostages so I could let go of my resentment.

I also reflected on the role that shame and embarrassment would have played in my mother's decision to keep it to herself. I wanted to hug her and console her and tell her it was okay. I wanted to tell her we all make mistakes. Sadly, I never had that opportunity, and, with her recent death, I never will.

My mother catalogued other history in the Bible, too. There was *Births*, where all of my brothers and sisters and I were listed; there was *Deaths*, where only my father's name and suicide date appeared; and there was *Membership Record*, which my mother left blank, probably because its meaning is unclear.

This very Bible ended up playing an important role in my life after I turned thirty-five. It was then that I underwent much religious study, spiritual advising, and praying, and experienced a religious conversion. Since that transformation, I have carried my father's Memorial Bible and read it often. It has been a portal for me to better understand Jesus' life from the moment of conception, through His public ministry, and finally to His Resurrection and Ascension. Reading His teachings about living a virtuous life and suffering on the cross has not only helped me move beyond my father's suicide, it has helped me find inner joy.

I continue to feel uneasy about my mother's catalogued entries in the Bible, but I have also become grateful for them. The traumatic incidents we experienced as a family are blatantly missing, making that recorded rendition incomplete, foreign, and chilling to me at times. Their absence makes my family appear like a textbook perfect TV family from the fifties.

Of course, that is a lie.

We were not a cohesive family, not even when we all lived under one roof. Dad was out drinking with his buddies and flirting and fooling around with his female followers. He spent all our money on them and on his booze. He never gave any of it to us for day-to-day subsistence. That was the real story. But I made my mother the scapegoat because she was the one who filled in the blanks, and she was the one who was physically present with us.

With time, I came to see that my mother wasn't to blame for the misrepresentation of our family. A Memorial Bible just isn't the place to sort out family strife. Its absence, however, presents a little irony: The book of Truth is left saddled with a reminder of lies of omission.

Memorable Minutiae Four

During his teen years, my father entertained his friends by doing handstands on the railings of the high diving board at the local public swimming pool. I was a gymnast and was quite acrobatic. My brother Don told me when he came home on leave from the army and searched out my father, my father would mention that he saw photos of me in the *Union Leader*, the local city newspaper. I was doing handstands at a city event or getting an award at a meet. When Don told me about those exchanges, I felt special for a fleeting moment.

During those times Don came home on leave from the army and searched out my father, he usually found him drinking in one of the downtown bars. I'm not sure my father always had a place of residence.

5

The Family Legacy

People often think of family legacy in terms of material goods passed from one generation to another. Money in the bank, a life insurance payout, grandma's old clock, and the antique piano come to mind. Legacy, however, refers to intangibles as well: a grandmother's legacy of love and respect, a legacy at a university, and a legacy of pain from the Great Depression. I never considered something as horrific as suicide to be a legacy, but the concept emerged more clearly during my research for this book.

I found its oppressive force contaminating past and current generations of my family tree, and I became suspicious that it was a factor in the unfolding of our genealogy. By no means is suicide a desirable family legacy, but it is a real one. In a relatively brief thirty-year time span in my family, there were two suicides, one nonfatal suicide attempt, and four ongoing battles against its mental and physical torment. The historical recount is below.

1945 – My father's father died in a boating incident. Some family members thought he committed suicide, but most of the information supports a drowning.

1983 – My father died by suicide via hanging.

Circa 1980 – My cousin Mark died by suicide using a shotgun.

1992 – My cousin Angela's daughter, Ruth, died by suicide using a gun.

1999 – One of my sisters battled suicidal ideation.

2000 – I attempted suicide via an overdose and also had oppressive struggles with suicidal ideation.

2013 – Ethan, another cousin, told me he and his sister Claire battled oppressive suicidal ideation over the years. At least one of them is known to struggle with it today.

When I saw so many suicides and suicide-related incidents in such a short period in our family history, I was unnerved. This was the family legacy my sons were inheriting! I became more motivated to forge them a new legacy, one of life and living. I became more determined to beat my own struggles.

Simultaneously, in a strange perhaps perverse twist, the suicide-tainted family history provided me with fleeting relief. I discovered I wasn't alone. It's not that I would wish illness upon anyone, but the knowledge alleviated some of the isolation I was experiencing.

I searched on the Internet and in the library for articles about suicide. In one, the researchers found that people with suicide in their family history were at a 2.1-fold increased risk of completing suicide as well. They also found that when a family member took his own life, the resulting suicide rate in first-degree relatives, e.g., parent, sibling, child, was three-and-a-half times greater than the resulting suicide rate in first-degree relatives who are still alive. This is a definite cause for concern in my family.

The phenomenon of having multiple completed or attempted suicides fall within a relatively short time period is called familial clustering or intergenerational suicide. As shown in the study above, families with clustering are at significantly higher risk of suiciding than families without it. If family members know this information, however, they can improve their situation with direction for better living, and hopefully with specific ways to avoid suicidal behavior.

It is akin to people who inherit diabetes or have certain forms of cancer. When they learn their family history, they can live more judiciously. I can do the same. I must do the same. I cannot afford to ignore the presence of this illness in my life if I want a new family legacy for my sons.

SUSPECTED SUICIDE – *My Grandfather*

After my father committed suicide, my brother Don told me our grandfather did the same. He said one of our uncles had told him Pépère put on "cement shoes" and jumped out of his boat while he was fishing on a local lake.

I didn't become curious about this story until several years later. I was reviewing my family history again in therapy, and I wanted confirmation on what my brother had told me. So I wrote to my paternal grandmother, my Mémère. A few months lapsed and I still hadn't heard from her. I wondered if she was upset with me for bringing up the subject.

Not long after that, I received a letter from one of my father's brothers, Jerry. He and I had exchanged occasional letters over the years, so I thought it was another one in our sequence. As I read it, though, I quickly realized it was different. He mentioned the letter I had written to my grandmother and said he was responding in her stead. She was getting up there in years and was too fragile to talk about my grandfather's death.

I was excited about finally knowing what happened, but that dissipated quickly when I realized my uncle was avoiding my questions about my grandfather's death. I couldn't believe he would do such a thing, so I reread the letter a few more times. I was disappointed and frustrated when I didn't find any reference to my grandfather's death. It was stunning and I was left empty-handed. I couldn't help but suspect that my grandfather committed suicide. Why else would my uncle avoid the subject? I figured he must have been too ashamed to discuss the details. Unfortunately, he is no longer living. Perhaps like many survivors of suicide (those left behind by the one who died via suicide), he didn't have the emotional preparedness to talk about it openly.

So I called Don. This time, which was many years later, he couldn't recall the details of his exchange with our uncle who had told him our grandfather's death could have been a suicide. He couldn't remember which uncle told him this snippet of our family history. Accidental drowning was the only method for which there was sustainable evidence, so I couldn't say he died by suicide.

In 2012, I connected with my cousin Angela on Facebook, and I became hopeful again that I might know more about what happened to my grandfather. Angela suggested I talk with her mother, my Aunt Lorraine, who was my father's oldest sister, as well as the oldest sibling in their family. I took Angela's suggestion. When I called my aunt, she was more than eighty years old.

Our conversation was pleasant and fruitful. I learned quite a bit about her and our family. She still goes bowling every week and does her exercises. She is convinced that her exercises have been the key to prolonging her ability to walk and bowl and generally function without a walker or a cane. She was divorced early on and still lives in the house she bought twenty years ago. When her children were young, Aunt Lorraine worked in the school cafeteria, and later, in a factory. She was open about her mother and father.

When she told me that her mother was born in my hometown of Manchester and her father was born in Canada, I felt disconnected. I never knew these facts about my grandparents.

Neither did I know that my grandmother went to school in Canada or that they owned a nine-unit apartment building and lived in one of the units with their children.

I was saddened to hear that my grandmother couldn't take care of the apartment building after my grandfather died. She had to sell it and buy a smaller home. That is the home I knew—the home where I spent time visiting her. While my grandfather was still living, there was a period when they needed more money to sustain themselves, so my grandmother took a job outside the home. For her to do that, though, someone had to stay home with the children. My grandparents chose Aunt Lorraine. They told her she had to drop out of high school when she was fifteen years old. To this day, my aunt regrets that she never received her high school diploma.

She said she was upset when my father was born. She didn't appreciate the new baby who was getting a lot of attention in the house. I could identify with her jealousy, since I experienced it with my brothers and sisters. Aunt Lorraine said she was so mad at first that she didn't even look at my father, but with time, she learned to coddle him like everyone else did. She even became enamored with him. She would hold him and call him Petit Ange Noir, which translates to Little Black Angel, a name stemming from his dark skin, even at a very young age.

Aunt Lorraine also revealed that my father was a handful, such that my grandmother couldn't keep up with his active nature. She couldn't even catch him to wipe his nose. My aunt often did the task, since my father went more readily to her than to my grandmother.

Apparently, my father's rambunctiousness was a major contributor to my grandparents' decision to place him in a nearby orphanage, which acted like today's version of daycare. It was common for parents to get help from them to better manage their households. Nonetheless, I was saddened because my father was in an institution at a very young age, often apart from the rest of his family. Some called children in that situation a part-time orphan.

While he was there, he received schooling. My grandmother attended a teacher's meeting once; it was then that she first learned how smart my father was. Emotionally, though, he had a difficult time adjusting, and he was brought home full time within the year. Somehow that doesn't seem like it was soon enough, but I know how easy it can be to misjudge circumstances from a distance.

My grandfather became very attached to my father, and he took him everywhere he went. Naturally, when my grandfather died, my father was deeply affected by the loss. He was eight years old and was never the same afterward. Aunt Lorraine said he was often sad, and I thought, *I bet he was*.

When I asked her about my grandfather's death, she was quite definitive in saying he died from accidental drowning. She remembered the day well, because he was supposed to pick her up after one of her activities. She called my grandmother when he didn't show up at the railroad station, and my grandmother told her to take a taxi, which is what she did.

Eventually, Aunt Lorraine explained that my grandfather had gone fishing that day. She said most of my other aunts and uncles would tell a similar story. She had been told that the waters became unexpectedly rough that day, and when they did, my grandfather leaned over to start the motor so he could head back home. At that point, they believe his sweater got caught on the motor, which then fell off the boat and pulled him in. My aunt said the family waited and waited to hear something from the authorities, but it was ten days before my grandfather's body was found. I struggled for words as she ended our conversation by telling me she moved to Rhode Island when she was eighteen years old.

I was quite grateful to have spoken with my aunt. Her voice put a human touch on my father's childhood and on my grandfather's life. Our discussion filled in holes I didn't even know existed. The experience was enriching, even with the small glimpse my aunt gave me into my father's life and his siblings and parents when they were growing up. I finally understood why people spend so much time researching their genealogy.

My heart went out to Aunt Lorraine when she told me she unwillingly dropped out of high school to take care of her brothers and sisters. She had completed her freshman year and wanted to continue but couldn't. When she described my father's confinement in the orphanage, I felt great sadness again, not just for him but also for the entire family. It was evident from her story that the siblings were close.

Aunt Lorraine's honesty about her reaction to my father's birth was moving and real. She brought my heritage to life and I yearned to connect with each of my relatives. As I thought about my grandfather's death and the ten days before they found his body, I imagined the suffering my grandmother and all her children must have endured. The heart-wrenching wait and the final discovery of my grandfather's body was probably nothing less than torturous.

Since my grandfather was missing for so long, I wondered if there might be a newspaper article or police report about him, so I did some research. The police department didn't have records from that far back, so I focused my efforts on finding a newspaper article. I searched through microfiche at his local public library, and my jaw dropped when I saw the first article. My hunch was right. When I came out of my mild stupor, I forged forward with the search and found four more articles. That was five altogether. Some are presented here.

The newspaper articles clearly state that my grandfather's boating incident was an accidental drowning. I certainly lean in that direction, but there are some details that leave me perplexed.

- ॐ The very first newspaper article says my grandfather had a companion when he rented the boat, yet that companion is never mentioned in any of the four articles that follow. Where did that companion go? Why wasn't he ever mentioned again? Maybe he murdered my grandfather. Maybe it was a "she" and not a "he." That would put a different twist on everything.

- ॐ How about that can of gasoline found under the boat while there was no motor found?

- ॐ Aunt Lorraine said there were rough waters that caused my grandfather to try to start the motor. Rough waters were never mentioned in the newspapers, and the lake is small and not typically associated with rough waters. Were the waters indeed rough, or is that just what my grandmother and other adults told my aunt?

- ॐ If my grandfather had his own outboard motor, why didn't he have his own boat? Why did he have to rent one? Aunt Nancy filled in the answers for these questions for me. She told me my grandfather had no garage to store a boat, so he bought his motor and rented boats when he went fishing. It was a common thing to do back then.

These details surrounding his death will most likely never be resolved, and without more conclusive evidence that my grandfather took his own life, I can't conclude that he committed suicide.

Article courtesy of the *Union Leader*, Manchester, NH

TEXT

Drag for Fisherman, May 21, 1945 – "State Police started this morning to drag for the body of George Laplante of... street, who went fishing in a rowboat in Lake...Saturday morning and disappeared. The boat he rented for fishing was found floating upside down between Deer Neck and Rocky Point but there was no trace of Laplante. It is in this area that dragging operations started with Troopers... and... directing the search. Dennis Mòrisette, who rented the boat to Mr. Laplante, said that the Manchester man and a companion came to him Saturday asking for a boat. 'I didn't want to rent one,' said the boat owner, 'as I hadn't finished working on those I had. The boat they wanted didn't have any oarlocks or oars. However, Laplante said he didn't need the oars because he had an outboard motor.' Park Vaughan, who found the boat, said that a can of gasoline was under the boat but the motor was gone."

Drag for Fisherman

State Police started this morning to drag for the body of George Laplante of .... street who went fishing in a rowboat in Lake Massabesic Saturday morning and disappeared.

The boat he rented for fishing was found floating upside down between Deer Neck and Rocky Point but there was no trace of Laplante. It is in this area that dragging operations started with Troopers Clifton Smith, Emil Dion and James Brown directing the search.

Dennis Mòrisette, who rented the boat to Mr. Laplante, said that the Manchester man and a companion came to him Saturday asking for a boat.

"I didn't want to rent one," said the boat owner, "as I hadn't finished working on those I had. The boat they wanted didn't have any oarlocks or oars. However, Laplante said he didn't need the oars because he had an outboard motor."

Park Vaughan, who found the boat, said that a can of gasoline was under the boat but the motor was gone.

Two days after my grandfather went fishing. May 21, 1945.

Article courtesy of the *Union Leader*, Manchester, NH

Ten days after my grandfather went fishing.
May 29, 1945.

Body found face upward, still wearing watch and glasses.

TEXT

Find Body of George Laplante in Lake. "The body of George A. Laplante of... street, father of seven children, who was drowned 10 days ago in Lake Massabesic while boat fishing, was recovered about 9 o'clock Tuesday morning off Rocky Point.

The body was discovered floating face upward on the surface, a short distance east of Deerneck bridge on the Londonderry turnpike. The point was approximately one-half mile south, searchers said, of the spot where Laplante's overturned boat was picked up at 4:30 p.m. on May 20, the day following disappearance of the Queen City man.

Death by accidental drowning was the verdict issued by Dr. Francis B. King of Derry, Rockingham county medical referee, after viewing the body. It had been in the water about 10 days, the condition indicated, the referee stated. Laplante's watch was found on his person, practically run down, with the hands pointing to 2 o'clock. Laplante's glasses, unbroken, were still in place."

SUICIDE #1 – *My Father*

My father committed suicide when he was forty-five years old, the same age as his father was when he died in his boating accident. Their identical age at death could have been a coincidence or it could have been part of a larger cycle of abandonment in our family tree. Either way, the end result can feel like abandonment. My father was on the receiving end when he was put in the orphanage and again when my grandfather died. My brothers and sisters and I were on the receiving end when my father went out drinking, withheld money from the family, hit my mother, was verbally inappropriate with us, and of course, when he took his own life.

My siblings and I, my mother, and my father's girlfriend were left in the wake of his self-destruction to assimilate it all. The police officers who arrived and reported the incident, the doctor who declared his death to be suicide, my uncle Édouard who was called to the scene, and many more people in the community were also affected. Thirty-two years have passed and the assimilation continues.

SUICIDE #2 – *My Cousin Mark*

Several years after my father took his own life, my cousin Mark did the same. I believe it was in the 1980s and he was in his late twenties. One evening, he climbed to the top of Rock Rimmon ledge and shot himself. I don't know how he obtained the gun, but I do know he had been deeply depressed, living alone, and struggling for a long time. It is also possible that he was taking lithium medication and had gone off it. Since mental illness was in his mother's side of the family too, it is difficult to know how much each side contributed genetically to his mental health. Most likely, both sides contributed something.

SUICIDE #3 – *My Cousin Angela's Daughter Ruth*

In 1992, after being depressed for a period of time, my cousin Angela's daughter, Ruth, took her own life. She had become suspicious that her boyfriend was cheating on her. Through her own detective work, she discovered firsthand that he truly was betraying her. In a state of desperation, she shot and killed herself. Her mother Angela was devastated. After some time passed, she started a ministry in which the bereaved participants are invited to plant a tree and string on lights in memory of their loved one lost to suicide. Angela found the activity to be healing, and now provides healing for many others in similar situations.

NONFATAL SUICIDE ATTEMPT – *Me*

When my cousin Mark took his life, I was again awakened to the reality that my suicidal ideations could materialize, but I didn't take the prospect as seriously as I should have. Years later, I was deeply depressed and in an unbearable amount of emotional pain. I was struggling with work, my role as a mother, my social life, and finances. I was also distraught from the revolving-door treatment in emergency rooms mandated by my health insurance company. That approach had taken its toll and wore me down. With few family members or friends as resources, my depression escalated and I decided to disregard my previous resolution to stay alive for my Kegan and Alden's sakes.

I convinced myself that they had plenty of other adults who could and would raise them, and when they got older, they would be self-sufficient. This skewed assessment made it more justifiable to take my own life, not just ruminate about it. So I swallowed a few bottles of what I considered to be my most potent medications.

Today, as an adult, I am acutely aware of how much I need my father and how much children, in general, need their parents throughout their lives. During my crisis and overdose, though, I was unaware of or perhaps simply unable to recognize those dynamics. Thankfully, I awoke in my apartment and called my psychiatrist. He told me to get to the hospital, so I asked one of my neighbors to take me, and she did.

In the meantime, my psychiatrist called 9-1-1. When the paramedics arrived at my house, they used an ax to break through the lock on my apartment door, but no one was home. The responding team turned around and went back to their ambulance dispatch site.

I was answering questions for the admissions nurse in the emergency room and we were looking at each other in surprise. We had just realized I was passed out in my apartment for an entire day more than I knew. We discovered this when the nurse asked me to tell her the current day and date, and I gave her the ones for the day before. I had no idea what happened in those twenty-four hours, but the missing time still catches me by surprise when I think back on it.

After admission, the nursing staff gave me some activated charcoal to prevent further absorption of the medicine I used for the overdose. Constipation with hard and black stools was a painstaking side effect. Another uncomfortable consequence was having to talk to counselors and face the pain I wanted to avoid when I first took all those pills.

After I got through the discussions with the staff, I had a new internalization of the adage "Suicide is a permanent solution to a temporary problem." I could have been dead, gone, never to return, and it had just hit me. It markedly hit me again when I was finally discharged from the hospital and saw the remnants of the emergency responders' ax marks around my door lock. I felt a thud in my stomach. The damage was another reminder of how serious my circumstances were, but I didn't take them that way until then. I was embarrassed and ashamed, and I told no one in my family about any aspect of it. I told none of my friends and none of my neighbors. I certainly didn't tell my children, until now.

ONGOING SUICIDAL IDEATION #1 AND #2 –
One of My Sisters and Me

One day, I was talking to one of my sisters when our cousin Mark's suicide came up. She was depressed at the time and struggling herself. She wondered out loud if Mark had the right answer after all. She eventually denounced her hypothesis, but I remained sad and scared. It was disturbing for me to hear one of my own siblings express suicidal sentiments similar to the ones I often had, and to the ones my father and Mark must have had.

As I listened to her, my suicidal thinking became normalized. It was a risky transformation, because I then knew another family member was struggling with it, too. And my suicidal thoughts seemed more commonplace and less pathological. Suicide became more feasible and even more enticing.

"If she thinks that, and my father and Mark thought similar things, then suicide may not be as whacked out as the professionals want me to believe." That line of thinking frightened me, because even though I frequently deliberated suicide, deep down I didn't want to discover more catalysts that would trigger my mental state to go in that direction.

ONGOING SUICIDAL IDEATION #3 AND #4 –
My Cousins Ethan and Claire

Ethan and Claire are siblings. In 2013, Ethan approached me at a family gathering and said, "I heard you're writing a book."

"Yes, I am. Do you know what it's about?" I asked. He nodded. He told me he and Claire have struggled with depression and being suicidal throughout the years. He was doing well at the time, but he was concerned about his sister. He expressed that it was important that I write this book and he emphasized that people need to know that this happens. I agreed and was grateful my cousins were still alive.

Memorable Minutiae Five

When I was in grade school, my mother took us children to a local bar. She was picking up my dad and thought our presence would make him less tempted to do as he usually did, i.e., lag behind, drink some more, and leave my mother waiting. She was wrong. So she brought us from the car into the bar and sat us at a big table. An acquaintance of my father's came over and was playful with us. He offered to pay twenty-five cents to any of us who could push their right leg up and over their head onto the nape of their neck. I could do it, and I could do it repeatedly, so the man gave me twenty-five cents each time.   [Pride, Fun]

When I was in grade school, my mother took us children to a local bar. She was picking up my dad and thought our presence would make him less tempted to do as he usually did, i.e., lag behind, drink some more, and leave my mother waiting. She was wrong. So she brought us from the car into the bar and sat us at a big table. An acquaintance of my father's came over and was playful with us. He offered to pay twenty-five cents to any of us who could push their right leg up and over their head onto the nape of their neck. I could do it, and I could do it repeatedly, so the man gave me twenty-five cents each time.   [Shameful, Embarrassed]

6

My Unrelenting Ideation

During my darkest days with depression, my face was long and drab, expressionless. My voice was flat and my body had little animation. I often felt like my whole existence was in a deep freeze, cold and black. The only direction my mind could go was downward in a spiral. I persuaded myself that no one would be fazed by my committing suicide. I had little contact with my family and was convinced they all thought it was just a matter of time before I killed myself. I really believed no one cared—and that was true both during my marriage and after, when I was living on my own.

Interwoven with that sluggishness were pockets of fury and despair. "If I was a cutter, I'd cut my wrists right now," I told my therapist. "It's the only thing that'll alleviate my pain." Thankfully, I never did cut my wrists. I did, however, contend with an exhausting battle between invasive suicidal thoughts trying to convince me there was no hope and affirmative self-talk trying to convince me there was. My effort was often white knuckle in nature. I gritted my teeth while trying to persuade myself that what I knew through faith and reason was right, and what I knew through suicide and injury was wrong.

The two categories of thought would battle against each other in a duel-like fashion. I watched and listened in trepidation, and I was never certain of the outcome. Holding my breath, I asked myself, *"Is this the time I'm gonna do it?"* I was completely conscious of my mental state, yet too weak to loosen its hold. It was as if it was suspended right in front of me but just out of reach. I often had an illusory sense of power during those times. It was the power of free will, and it was palpable. Though I couldn't touch it in one instance, in another, I knew I could grab it by the throat and choose to end my life. All I had to do was go along with my suicidal thoughts and say the F-bomb to everyone. I would be done with it, and no one would have a say in the matter.

That was just one of my pockets of fury and despair. *I'm going to show them.* I'd get stuck in that molasses-like blackness for a while, but I never knew for how long. It always felt like time stood still. At some point, though, an affirmation-like thought would take hold. Sometimes it was a word, sometimes it was a whole sentence, sometimes it was an image. Like a hiccough, it would snap me out of my darkened obsession.

That now familiar statement of truth, "Suicide is a permanent solution to a temporary problem," helped me in a few ways during those crises. First, the phrase pertained directly to the situations I was in, and that was always helpful. Second, it provided an alternate perspective, highlighting the fact that there was no coming back after suicide. Once it's done, it's done.

A third reason this adage helped had to do with my inability to quickly process its meaning. Every time it came to me anew, I had to assimilate it again. I had to reconsider the definitions of the words permanent, solution, and temporary, and I had to think about how their meanings fit together. It took me time to visualize the different facets, to remember that it meant things can get better. One might think the delay could have been a problem, but in my case, those milliseconds made a difference. They either nudged me off suicide's doorstep or, if they kept me on it, they prevented me from jumping. From a spiritual perspective, I believe the delay allowed God and His angels to step in and protect me somehow.

This mental torment went on intermittently for many years. Early on, the darkness of suicide enveloped me such that I just wanted to stop the unending pain. I didn't care about the people I would leave behind, because if I cared about them, that might puncture the Berlin Wall inside me and open the floodgate to unending pain and grief. Taking my own life felt like it would provide more relief than facing my feelings ever could. They were that scary. I also battled my perceived abandonment by God. *If He didn't care, then who did? Why would He let this happen to me?* I lacked the vocabulary to describe my pain, and therein lay a major hindrance to healing. It was like going to the doctor for help and not being able to describe my ailments. The frustration exacerbated my despair.

The thoughts I had about wanting to die or kill myself arose not only when I was deeply depressed and hopeless, but also when I was more optimistic, because I knew it was just a matter of time before I would be in a state of despair again. These ruminations came when I was on medication, and they came when I was off. They were intermittent and subversive, impelling me to seriously consider jumping off a bridge, shooting myself with a gun (I didn't own one, but I thought I could buy one at the local firearms store), cutting myself with a knife, or suffocating myself in my car. In the end, though, I was unable to choose among those methods, so I never put a final plan together. Even my overdose was planned less than two hours before I took all the pills.

The time I did give in and take my pills, I came to understand the broader impact of suicide. I was trying to murder myself. That connection didn't register within me until then. After that, I realized that doing away with my own existence wasn't just about the elimination of one individual in a vacuum. It was about more than just me. That may seem obvious, but when I walked around in suicidal pain, I could barely see beyond myself. It was like hitting my thumb while hammering a nail. The pain was so immense and intense that I could think about nothing else.

After much therapy and discussion with others, the true nature of ending my life settled in my psyche. I would not only do away with the existence of me, I would also do away with the existence of my mother's daughter, my siblings' sister, my sons' mother, my grandchildren's grandmother, and my friends' and coworkers' comrade. The far-reaching tentacles of suicide became vividly and personally clear. Remorse and trepidation settled into my bones, and I finally felt some concern about the gaping hole I would leave in the family tree, like the one my father left.

A new resolve surfaced within me. Previously absent energy surged forth, and I became motivated to beat the odds associated with the cluster-like suicide pattern in my family. I wanted to disrupt my tragic family legacy and shield my sons from unwarranted suffering. I wanted to be there for them to show them that people hang around when they love you. They don't determine when their life will end; they let God do that.

I committed to taking responsibility for my life and breaking the family cycle. Unfortunately, my issues and suicidal ruminations didn't just disappear with my change in attitude. In fact, they were as active as before. Even when they lay dormant, they seemed to be seething, just waiting to take hold of my consciousness.

The fear I had of giving into suicide finally became greater than the control I felt from not talking about it, so I decided to disclose it to my therapist. When I did, I felt some relief. I felt further relief when I wrote about the different methods in my journal. I drew simple pictures showing how I would carry each one out. The scenes reflected intense anger and despair, primarily from feeling trapped about the lot I had received in life, including having to work so hard to stay alive by constantly overriding the irrational and frequently negative stream of ideas intruding upon my mental well-being.

There was one other facet that kept me on track with my commitment to my sons. It was a not-at-all altruistic notion: I should keep myself alive, because I might fail when I try to kill myself and I could then end up living in a worse state of life. *"What if I shoot myself in the head and miss the part of my brain that stays alive? I could end up paralyzed in a wheelchair. What if I jump from a bridge without reaching the velocity needed to kill myself? I could end up brain dead in a coma. What if I hang myself and someone finds me before the point of no return? I could suffer permanent damage from the noose and lack of oxygen."* These what-if scenarios were real deterrents because they were real possibilities. I saw them manifested in other patients at the hospital and they reminded me that I didn't have control over anything, not even my own death.

Long before I read about the legacy effects of suicide, my therapist told me that children of a parent who committed suicide are at higher risk of committing suicide themselves compared to children who are never exposed to such a trauma. I looked at him, thinking he was an idiot (my mindset back then) for telling me this. "That's supposed to make me feel better?" I groaned. He told me he was concerned for my safety and was trying to get me to take my situation seriously. I told him that information made me feel like I was fighting a losing battle.

I continued. "Good, then it's just a matter of time and I'll be gone. No more pain, no more therapy, no more crazy life. I can't wait. Just take me, the sooner the better." I felt a strange sense of relief "knowing" it was just a matter of time before my life was ended. I would no longer have to make sense of the conflicting thoughts clashing around in my head: Irrational one minute, reasonable the next, simple, then complicated, congenial, then outright vicious. The idea of being free of the torment was appealing. My therapist's information backfired, at least temporarily.

Revealing these inner most thoughts, i.e., my "secrets," to my therapist, left me feeling like I lost control and lost any psychological footing I may have perceived myself to have. My heart sank and then raced in fear. Even though that kind of loss was a step toward health, it felt like I was quashing my free will, and there was no way I was going to do that. It was a step closer to relinquishing my last resort, suicide, and no one was going to take that away from me.

Years later, I learned about a coping strategy people use at any stage of a suicidal crisis. It is called a suicide safety plan. I have wondered if such a plan would have helped deter me from my overdose. The plan is a list that begins with basic aids and moves to increasingly more elaborate ones. The person compiles it with their therapist, and they keep it in a safe and easy-to-access place. By shifting their focus from their intense emotions to ways of keeping themselves safe, it is thought that people with plans are more apt to reduce the likelihood of acting on their impulses. Here is a generic example:

1) If depressed and headed into the psychological space where suicidal thoughts arise, do something calming, like take a hot shower, go for a walk, or listen to music.

2) If the depressive mental state continues, call a trusted friend or family member. (List names and phone numbers here. Talk it over with them first.)

3) Tell myself what I would tell a friend who was considering suicide.

4) If suicidal thoughts become obsessive, remove from the house all guns, ropes, pills, and anything that is life threatening. Give them to someone safe and call my therapist.

5) If symptoms persist such that I am consumed with pain and suicidal impulses, call 9-1-1 or ask my neighbor to drive me to the closest emergency room.

As the intensity of a suicidal crisis grows, the intensity of the actions needed to prevent that suicide also grows. That is why having the strategy in writing beforehand is beneficial. A person can then stay more grounded to better manage their symptoms and more readily reach out to others for help.

Memorable Minutiae Six

My father enjoyed playing games. In addition to chess, he played an advanced game of Solitaire. He taught me how to play, and to this day, I still play the game. Some of my sisters do as well. I enjoy it and think of him every time I play.

I can only recall one instance when my father gave my brothers and sisters and me money. He did it posthumously through a life insurance policy. After the insurance company finished their administrative tasks, they forwarded us each a check for a small amount. I don't know how that transpired, since life insurance companies don't usually pay out on suicides.* Nonetheless, I was grateful to get help with paying my bills. Today, I would forego the money in exchange for a sober father who was involved in my life.

---

* As seen in this excerpt from my father's obituary, his suicide was not mentioned.

Article courtesy of the *Union Leader*,
Manchester, NH, January, 1983

Roger D. Laplante

Roger D. Blackie Laplante,
45, of   St., died at his residence Monday evening after a
short illness.

If this misrepresentation was communicated to the life insurance company, it makes sense that they would have paid out on his policy.

7

My Birthday

Nothing in the world can change the fact that our two events came together on January 24, 1983. My father's death by suicide and my birthday were intimately woven forever. Even now, more than thirty years later, I become perplexed when I think about this perverted expression of providence. I have no idea why God would allow such a horrible thing to happen. Through my faith, though, I know He allows each of us to exercise our own free will, and sometimes that ends up in tragedy. To deal with the fallout of this aberration, I started repeating a mantra at one point.

"My father committed suicide on my birthday."
"My father committed suicide on my birthday."

It evolved into something like a Native American vision quest, or an Australian Aborigine walkabout. My mantra became the vehicle in which I transported myself into the wilderness. Once there, I underwent a journey in which I searched for personal meaning that would take me into adulthood. Unlike the Native Americans or Australian Aborigines, however, I never quite made it to the other side, i.e., to integration. So I continued to rely on my mantra for grounding.

While I did homework, washed dishes, worked, carried my sons in the grocery store parking lot, and stretched at the yoga studio, I wondered if my father took his own life on my birthday because he felt some melancholic connection to a life he missed out on. *"Was he depressed because he was never emotionally or spiritually connected to our family, a family he was instrumental in creating? Or was he depressed due to sad circumstances in his own life? Why did it all come to a head in January on my birthday that year? Was he drunk? Was he thinking about me as he prepared the belt/ noose? I wonder if he even knew it was my birthday."*

I talked to myself like that from time to time, knowing I'd never receive answers, but the repetitive nature of the self-talk soothed me. At one point, I decided to break the silence within my family, only to become frustrated, disappointed, and quite lonely when I heard the replies: "No way. Dad didn't do that. He didn't intentionally hang himself on your birthday. Your birthday had nothing to do with it. The two aren't even related. He never remembered any of our birthdays."

"They just don't get it," I said to myself as I wept.

They had a point about my father not remembering our birthdays. He never telephoned or sent cards, but I had a hard time believing he would forget everything. Wanting to protect him, and the scenario mulling around in my head, I suggested he could have remembered our birthdays over the years; he just might not have done anything for them.

Having a mathematical mind, I turned to statistics. I knew I was grasping for straws, but I was desperate. I determined that the raw statistical odds of my father hanging himself on that day in January of that year were one out of 365, or 0.274 percent. That meant, all things being equal, there was only a 0.274 percent chance that my father's suicide was a random event. Those odds are so low that some additional influence had to be present.

Unfortunately, it was difficult, and more likely impossible, to determine what that influence was. It could have been a sad association with my birthday and/or our family. It also could have been stress due to bad finances, a major depressive episode, or any combination of those. Stepping back, I realized it had been quite some time since I delved into statistics, so my math and logic probably didn't make much sense. The point, however, is that I believed there was some mathematically significant possibility that my birthday played a role in his suicide, and that allowed me to maintain inner calm when my family members outright denied any connection.

I felt minimized during those exchanges, as if they were saying, "You are making way too much of this. Dad had no idea he was killing himself on your birthday." I felt crushed. I cowered and remained silent. Then I ruminated: *How could they think the two were totally disconnected. Couldn't they at least acknowledge the possibility?"*

I became frustrated, allowing dark thoughts to dominate my mind once again. I convinced myself that I'd been handed a bag of bad goods, and no one else had. Then one day while writing this book, there was a break in that Berlin Wall inside me. I found myself considering the possibility that my mother and brothers and sisters were genuinely trying to make me feel better and were trying to make themselves feel better as well. Who could blame them? After all, that is what I was trying to do for myself.

In the past, I believed they were in denial, but at that time, I came to believe they may have justifiably been exhibiting a sign of caring. That insight helped me to forgive them and release some of the anger I harbored toward them. I'm so glad for that, because later on, they confirmed that their intention really was to make me feel better.

Each year when my birthday came around, my mother and my brothers and sisters called to say happy birthday. I was grateful for their greetings, but I also yearned for someone to break the ice and at the very least, mention my father or his suicide, the proverbial elephants in the room. Since I was compelled to talk about them, I attended Al-Anon Adult Child meetings and poured out my heart to fellow travelers along the twelve-step path. I became grateful to Bill Wilson and Bob Smith, the founders of Alcoholics Anonymous. All other twelve-step spinoffs owe their existence to these two men, and in some ways, I feel like I owe my own personal existence to them as well.

I also took advantage of counseling to manage the intensity of my birthdays. While there, I more fully recognized and acknowledged the extent of my childhood deprivation. I realized I never had an explicit yearning for a father like my brother Don did. He experienced heartbreak after heartbreak when he longed for my father's presence at his activities, but my father never showed up. I, on the other hand, didn't consciously yearn for a father to be by my side, helping me with homework, coming to gymnastics meets, giving me a hug before bed, and even reprimanding me.

When I was awakened to the natural longings that children innately learn to manage at a young age, I came to know in my heart that I deserved time with my father, and on a more basic level, I deserved to have the yearning itself to be with him, the yearning that Don had. When that foreign way of existence settled into my bones, I came to know that therapy wasn't just a matter of drumming up emotions to keep my therapist in business. It was a matter of delicately reconnecting the parts of my psyche that got spattered into the universe during my childhood.

Also through therapy, I realized there was a link between my father's abandonment and my inability to trust and befriend others. Since my dad repeatedly abandoned me, that experience resided deep in the cells of my body. I was left with an unreasonable impulse to flee when relationships became challenging or other intense situations developed. Now that I understand the dynamic, though, I can override it. I can draw upon the virtues of perseverance and patience to stay engaged with people in all kinds of relationships and situations. Life has become a lot more interesting, and suicide has become a lot less interesting. It has even become unpalatable.

When I returned to the Catholic Church, I benefited from the solace provided in Her Sacraments and spiritual perspective. They helped me manage my residual frustration and disappointment. And as is always the case with good therapy and twelve-step programs, they helped me to see through a loving discovery of my own shortcomings that I had a part in creating the discord in my family. I wish I could say I was gentle with my shortcomings, and myself, but I wasn't. In fact, I hated myself, and it took a lot more work (and play) to put them all in their appropriate perspective. As I did that, I had a revelation that my family couldn't possibly understand what I was contending with. After all, my father committed suicide on *my* birthday, not on theirs. I needed to lower my expectations.

The door in my heart opened further, and I was able to see that my mother and my brothers and sisters could have been right about the coincidental timing of my father's suicide. I felt a calming sense of forgiveness come over me, not only toward them, but also toward my father—and me. And today, the Berlin Wall inside me continues to crumble. I never would have guessed that making myself more vulnerable would make me stronger in the end.

I was thankful for the resolution, but I was also saddened by the stark reality it represented. It confirmed that my father never had a substantive relationship with me, not at age nine, not at age seventeen, not on the day he died. He never cared about me. Although these revelations weren't original, my poignant experience of their probable accuracy and finality was. The associated torment pierced me, and I could barely catch my breath for a time. When I likened my agony to what Jesus must have felt when His executors scourged Him before hanging Him on the cross, His courage and ability to bear that pain provided me strength and solace to bear my own.

As demeaning as my father's neglect and abuse were, I found myself minimizing them at times. I would tell myself things like, *"Well, he wasn't able to care for me. He was sick. He was without faith, and he was weak. He needed help because he was a lost soul."* In reality, he was all that, but he also was guilty of inexcusable behavior. It took time and a lot of introspection to assign the appropriate blame upon him.

In more recent days, I have wondered if I was unconsciously harboring a remnant of desperate hope over the years. It was the hope that my father would finally notice me and consider me to be special in his eyes. I wondered if my pining for his attention fueled my drawing an exaggerated connection between his suicide and my birthday. I don't think about that possibility a great deal though.

For years after my father's suicide, my birthday loomed over me. Instead of celebrating my birth, I ruminated about his death, and I was often filled with great apprehension. When the day arrived, it was ominous and somber and I was sobbing much of the time. It took more than ten years for the intensity to die down. That is when my dad's suicide was no longer the center of attention on my birthday, and I was able to enjoy myself on my special day. The elephant in my family's living room had finally morphed into the skeleton in our family closet.

When I realized that even if there was no intentional connection between my father's day of death and my day of birth, the fact that the two coincided was eerie enough to justify the grieving I underwent. And that revelation was another step in the acceptance process.

Memorable Minutiae Seven

My father acted responsibly at times. He signed some of the parental approval lines on my report cards in elementary school. I still have them.

When my siblings and I entered our teenage years, Aunt Nancy threw birthday parties for my grandmother. She was getting on in years and my aunt wanted us to treasure our time with her. We always had great fun, especially with a swimming pool in the backyard. My father was alive during those years, but he was never present at any of the parties.

8

The Quest for Treatment

My medical treatment has involved lots of red tape. I have spent far too much time going around in circles trying to get definitive answers from health insurance companies, doctors' offices, and former employers, about coverage and payment. Unanswered phone calls, unreturned calls, being directed to the wrong department, and dealing with inflexible personnel, were just some of the debilitating red tape I battled.

At times, I've wondered if my father might still be alive if he had been able to get medical attention. But after going through the demanding and messy logistics of obtaining and navigating medical insurance for office visits, blood tests, medication, and visits with specialists, I have my doubts.

When I was twenty-nine years old, my husband and I lived in New Hampshire where he worked. I worked in Massachusetts in a high-tech job. At some point, my company relocated my work group further away from our home and my commute grew to one hour and twenty minutes one way. Since I was working only three days a week, the extra travel burden was manageable for a while. In time, however, it became too much, and we had to decide if we were going to move. That meant we had to figure out which one of us was going to keep his or her job. The decision was torturous.

After giving it much consideration, we decided to move to Massachusetts. We also decided to keep both jobs, which meant my husband had to absorb the one-hour-and-twenty-minute commute. Thankfully, like me, he was able to arrange to work part-time at three days per week.

At the time of our decision, we assumed I would be able to easily interview and hire a new therapist and psychiatrist in Massachusetts. We were wrong. After interviewing several, I hadn't found a satisfactory level of comfort with any of them. In the end, I decided to continue the almost three-hour round trip to see the therapist I had been working with in New Hampshire. I had a dependable rapport with him, and I didn't want to disrupt the stability of my treatment. We decided to meet once per week.

After doing that for several years, the commute became unbearable. My husband and I went through a divorce, and I struggled to keep up my performance at work. At the same time, my unrelenting depression made it difficult for me to stay focused, and both factors impeded my ability to parent well. When it came to thinking about parental custody, my husband and I decided to have our sons live primarily with their father. Technically, we shared physical custody evenly, but in practice, it was more like he was the custodial parent and I was the noncustodial parent. With respect to legal custody, we shared it evenly.

In the process, before the divorce was finalized, my husband moved back to New Hampshire with the boys. I agreed to it, but it meant several additional three-hour, round-trip commutes for me to spend time with Kegan and Alden each week. I also had my usual trip for therapy and medication appointments and I made the same commute each time I attended one of my son's school events and picked them up for their weekends with me.

I quickly became worn out. I knew if I wanted to save my driving for my sons' activities, I would have to find local Massachusetts providers for my therapy and medication management. Moving back to New Hampshire was not an option for me. I had built a support network where I was living, and it would have been destabilizing to establish a new one from ground zero. So I interviewed psychologists and psychiatrists in Massachusetts again. In doing so, I realized I would do best under one provider. That is, my treatment would progress best with one person doing both my therapy and overseeing my medication. That meant I had to find a psychiatrist. No other professional could fulfill the duty.

The glitch, however, was that health maintenance organizations (HMOs) had since subjugated psychiatrists to doing fifteen-minute medication checks with patients, while they paid psychologists and social workers to take over all therapy. Since these mental health providers were paid a lower rate than psychiatrists, the HMO appeared to be keeping costs down, which was its primary goal. If patients went outside that paradigm, however, the HMO wouldn't pay the extra cost, even if it meant they saved money in the long run.

Having medication checkups separate from therapy added an extra layer of interpersonal stress and commute time for me, and that hindered my psychological progress. Left with inadequate care, I would require longer-term treatment and drive up costs for the HMO.

Some people were quick to say, "Too bad. That's what the insurance policy says it will cover," but I didn't let their opinion hinder me. I knew about the appeal process. I think all HMOs have one. So I submitted a written appeal to my HMO and asked for an exception to their treatment mode. I explained how it would save them money in the long run.

The HMO denied my appeal, but it turned out that the denial was only at the initial level. They had another level beyond that, so I resubmitted my request to that level. Regrettably, it was denied there as well. I then submitted it to the last level, where their upper management approved my request to consolidate my treatment under one provider. The whole process took about a year.

I was so relieved. I started searching right away for a new psychiatrist. There weren't many who did both therapy and medication. It seemed that most had lowered their expectations for their role in the mental health treatment field and complied with fifteen-minute medication checks. Others felt it was a disservice to their patients, and they discontinued their contracts with the insurance companies. They found other ways to do business with clients, primarily by self-pay for those who could afford it.

I eventually found a doctor in the HMO network with whom I was comfortable. He was skilled at both therapy and medication. Unfortunately, he didn't have an opening in his practice. Time went by and I entered suicidal crisis again. I saw him at the hospital while trying to get help, and he fortuitously had an opening that time. I gladly switched from the ineffective therapist/psychiatrist tag team to this one doctor for everything. After twelve years, I am still with him. I reduced my commute time for appointments, I received the therapeutic stability I couldn't find in the piecemeal approach, and I was able to spend more time with my sons. It was a win-win for everyone involved, including the HMO.

Memorable Minutiae Eight

My father used to bounce me on his knee and pretend to steal my nose. It was one of the few ways he played with me when I was young. He would lightly pass his fist over my nose and on return, he would put his thumb between his forefinger and middle finger. Then he would hold up his hand and tell me he got my nose, as if he had just taken it off my face. Giggling uncontrollably, I really believed my nose was gone. *"How did he do that?"* I would wonder in delight.

One time, my father came home and sat in one of our kitchen chairs. I was fifteen years old. He inappropriately harassed and harped on my sister Lynn about her recent prom date. She was seventeen. Don was on the second floor. He was eighteen and heard the harangue coming from the lower level. He dashed down the stairs to protect Lynn. When he arrived in the kitchen, he walked up to my father and told him, "I think it's time for you to go now." My father stood up and stared into my brother's eyes. He was jarred when he saw that my brother had gone through a growth spurt and was a bit bigger and taller than he expected. Afraid of what might happen, my dad turned and left by the front door.

9

Further Investigation

Once I became situated with my new psychiatrist in Massachusetts, he suggested I take a further look at my family of origin. I wanted nothing to do with that idea. I had done a lot of introspection and therapy about the influence of my family on my life. I felt no need to do more. Since my psychiatrist knew the importance of personal readiness for tackling sensitive issues, he let this topic subside.

Years later, though, I developed an unexpected yearning to know more about my father. I was completely surprised by this development, but my psychiatrist wasn't. He knew that important topics weave in and out of ongoing therapy.

I decided to do some research to find more concrete details about my father's death. The first point of investigation was the nature of his death. Over the years, my mother and my brothers and sisters had begun to question the circumstances of his death. Financial strain was mentioned in the police report, so they wondered if his roommate or someone else to whom he might owe money might have killed him.

Their postulation was later intensified when my sister Diane hired a contractor to do some home renovations. The contractor had another man helping him, who after seeing my sister's last name, asked if she was related to Blackie. Blackie was a well-known nickname for my father—an adult version of his childhood nickname, Petit Ange Noir. When my sister told the employee that Blackie was her father, he revealed that he always doubted my dad died by suicide. He suspected it was a murder by the person to whom he owed money. He just didn't believe my father would take his own life.

With nothing more definitive to make a conclusion, murder remained an option. So I called the state medical examiner's (ME) office. I wanted to see if an autopsy was performed. The associated report might give us new insight. Unfortunately, the ME office

Page 1 of the police report.
Some identifying items have been grayed out.

couldn't find the file. They said either no autopsy was done or the records were lost several years ago when the office was moved to a new city. The medical examiner suggested I contact the police department for the police report, which I did.

The report was still on file. I became excited and nervous and scared. *"What would it say? Would it be too gory?"* I arranged to pick up a copy. It had been more than twenty years since my father's death, and I was quite rattled when I saw it. It was sterile in appearance and in tone. For some reason, I expected it would be a bit warmer; after all, they were talking about a human being.

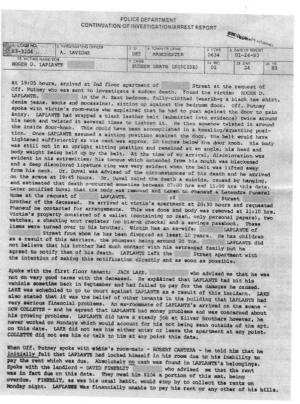

Page 2 of the police report.
Some identifying items have been grayed out.

The police department, however, wasn't in the business of making readers feel at ease. Their protocol was objective science and newspaper-like reporting. "Just the facts ma'am."

All quotes are meant to reflect how the text appears in the police report..

I was repeatedly jolted as I read each line. To begin with, the document was a criminal report. "A criminal report?" I asked myself. "Who was the criminal and what was the crime?" I was confused.

It turned out my father was categorized as both the criminal and the victim. He was the "criminal" who committed the "crime" of "Sudden Death (Suicide)" and he was the "VICTIM" because he was the one murdered. That was the first time I ever thought of suicide as murder, and it made sense in biblical terms. After all, the fifth of the Ten Commandments says, "Thou shalt not kill," and that includes "Thou shalt not kill thyself."

As I continued down the report, I saw my birthday listed as the date of my father's suicide. "MONTH 1, DATE 24, YEAR 83." To see it in black and white in such a dispassionate report was chilling. The "WEAPON-TOOL" was "Belt," while "HOW ATTACKED (MO)" was "Subject hung him self [sic] with a black belt on the bedroom door knob." That hit like a lead balloon, causing me to take a deep breath before I continued reading.

"A fireman attempted to enter the bedroom but was unable to because of the fact that the body was against the door. The fireman then pushed the door open enough to see that there was a belt around his neck." What fireman? There was no mention of a fireman coming to the scene. Perhaps he was on a fire truck that was hailed along with the ambulance. "Laplantes [sic] room mate [sic] … tried to push the door open and it would not open. He felt that Laplante was holding it closed so he pushed it harder. He then observed Laplante's Right [sic] arm which was purple in color."

"LAPLANTE had wrapped a black leather belt (submitted into. evidence) twice around the inside door-knob. This could have been accomplished in a kneeling/squatting position. Once LAPLANTE assumed a sitting position against the door, the belt would have tightened sufficiently as his neck was approx. 10 inches below the door knob."

I kept reading. "... discoloration was evident in his extremities; his tongue which extended from his mouth was blackened and a deep discolored ligature rung was very evident when the belt was lifted away from his neck." "Dr. Duval was advised of the circumstances of his death... Dr. Duval ruled the death a suicide, caused by hanging, and estimated that death o-ccurred [sic] sometime between 07:00 hrs and 11:00 hrs this date."

I wondered if that doctor was still alive.

"Victim has an ex-wife...from whom he has been divorced at least 10 years. He has children as a result of this marriage, the youngest being around 20 YOA. [Uncle Édouard] did not believe that his brother had much contact with his estranged family but he agreed to notify them of his death."

I felt displaced. There I was again as part of my father's suicide story. It was a flashback to his wake, when my mother and brothers and sisters and I lined up to be the receiving line. We were so far removed from his life at that point that representing him as his family seemed alien. No, it seemed like a lie.

"The first floor tenant also stated that it was the belief of other tenants in the building that LAPLANTE had very serious financial problems. An ex-roommate of LAPLANTE's arrived at the scene... and he agreed that LAPLANTE had money problems and was concerned about his growing problems."

"LAPLANTE did have a steady job at [a beer distributor company] however..."

"... victim's room-mate... told him that he initially felt that

LAPLANTE had locked himself in his room due to his inability to pay the rent which was due."

"Absolutely no cash was found in LAPLANTE's belongings."

"Spoke with the landlord... who advised... that the rent was in fact due on this date."

"LAPLANTE was financially unable to pay his rent or any other of his bills."

When I realized my father was forty-five years old and still had minimal belongings, I was stopped short. He lived in a barren apartment and remained in financial trouble, just like he had been when he "lived" at home with us.

I relayed the information in the report to the medical examiner I spoke to earlier. She said she had no doubt my father died by suicide. She cited things like the way his body was hanging behind the door, keeping it closed; the belt wrapped around his neck; the discolorations in his extremities and the blackening of his tongue. These are all things she had seen during her time as a coroner and she was confident in her assessment. She also mentioned that it was common for men to commit suicide by hanging or shooting themselves, while women tend to use carbon monoxide poisoning or large quantities of pills.

I wanted to talk to my siblings about this new information, but I held off. I was fairly certain such a conversation would end in disruption, so I waited for more inner calm before I broached the subject.

When the timing was right, I mentioned the police report and the medical examiner's assessment to my sister, Lynn. We had grown close after college. We talked many Saturday mornings by phone while our husbands tended to our children. Sometimes we stayed in our bedrooms and talked for a couple hours. We talked about the challenges and joys of being a new mom, and the struggles of balancing high-tech jobs with the demands of keeping up the house. We talked about the difficulties of finding time alone with our husbands and about the admiration and awe we had for our mother, who raised six children all about a year apart.

We recognized that my mother had been in survival mode for so many years. She wasn't available to the extent we wanted emotionally, which added strain to our relationship and household. We spent a lot of time trying to make sense of the unhealthy dynamics in our family. We were trying to avoid repeating the detrimental patterns with our own husbands and children, and with each other.

We reflected on the picnics we used to go on, how smart and how drunk my father was, how heroic our mother was, and the times our neighborhood friends were catalysts in getting us to misbehave. We exchanged stories about the arguments we had and about our misguided attempts to one-up our siblings and each other.

Those talks with my sister were very special. We learned how to open up to each other and share our innermost feelings. We also learned how to treat one other with respect, and how to simply be with each other.

When I mentioned the police report and the medical examiner's opinions, we agreed on some things and disagreed on others. We respected each other and hung up in a spirit of caring and love. I was pleased I chose her to begin opening up about my recent investigations.

I was surprised when I shared my findings with other members of the family. The conversations went well. Enough years must have gone by to smooth over the tense edges, resulting in calmer conversation. We took time to listen to each other. The exchanges weren't perfect, but they were noteworthy. I was relieved I could finally talk with them about my dad. I relayed the medical examiner's opinion, and I dared bring up the notion that my father might have taken his own life due to some connection with my birthday. This time, my mother agreed with me. There was no more protection or denial on her part, so I felt another huge burden lifted.

My siblings started to ponder lingering questions about his death: "Maybe he was murdered. Maybe one of his creepy acquaintances murdered him. [My mother had gone to the police with this idea at the time of the incident. They told her to drop it.] Maybe he owed that person some money... How could he have strangled himself with just his belt on a doorknob? Could he really get leverage that way? He was probably drunk... He lived a miserable life for so long, why did he decide to end it then? Was there someone else in his apartment with him? Where was his girlfriend?" Unfortunately, we couldn't get definitive answers to most of the questions, but at least we talked openly with one another. And that was the more important achievement in my mind.

The police report and medical examiner's input were gruesome, but they brought me peace. They provided concrete information on which to rely when I struggled with the churning in my brain. Twenty years after my father's suicide, I was imbued with calm and confidence, something I never would have predicted when I began my research.

I filed the report away. When I took it out and reread it several years later, my initial instinct was to find something in it that proved my father didn't carry out that self-mutilating act. I still longed for evidence that he didn't take his own life. I initially thought I might be experiencing denial about my father's death, but I realized my reaction was a sign of health. It was an indication that at my core I still cared about and still wanted my father. I may have been ashamed of him, but my protective instinct for loving him remained.

As I perused the report this second time around, I once again saw that my father's rent was due on my birthday. That didn't make sense. Rents are normally due on the first or the fifteenth or the thirtieth of the month, not on the twenty-fourth. Why would his rent be due on the twenty-fourth? I could only think of obscure reasons, like the overdue rent was a carryover from previous months, and for some reason, my father had an agreement to pay that debt off on the twenty-fourth of January.

He always had problems managing money. I suppose he could have made an agreement with his landlord to pay the back rent, or some portion of the back rent, on the day he died by suicide. While this doesn't seem likely to me, it could at least be a possibility.

When I shared the police report with my brother Don, he shared his experiences in more detail. My heart went out to him. Soon after Manchester city officials cleared the suicide scene, he went to my father's apartment. Thankfully, he took a friend along. The two of them found the place bare with only condiments and a six pack of beer in the fridge and a few items of clothing strewn in his bedroom. Don thought the belt lying on my father's bed was the one he used to hang himself. The police report, however, said the belt was turned in as part of the investigation. This discrepancy has never been resolved.

Don and his friend looked at the doorknob on the inside of my father's bedroom. They couldn't believe he could have hanged himself from it. Don even sat below it and tried to play out the suicidal act. He said the doorknob hit him at the lower part of his neck, between his shoulder blades. I presented the findings from the police report and medical examiner. I told him it is known that people hang themselves from doorknobs.

To this day, when my brother recounts the story, he becomes choked up and shakes his head as he says, "You wouldn't believe it. You just wouldn't believe it." Tears well up in his eyes sometimes and he yearns for that dad he never had. Like me in the mausoleum wanting my father to know his grandchildren, my brother has said he has wanted that same thing for his children.

I can't imagine what it was like for Don in my father's apartment the day after his suicide. Neither can I imagine what it was like for him each time he searched out my father when he was on leave from the army. Just three months before my dad took his own life, Don came home from Europe where he was stationed. It was around Christmas time. As he did every time he came home, he sought my father out and found him at one of the local bars. While there, he recalled how my father never showed up for his Little League baseball games. He second-guessed himself and wondered if his perspective was skewed. He knew he could never quench his thirst for my father's time and closeness, so he wondered if perhaps he was expecting too much of him by thinking he should have been at most of Don's games.

Remembering those painful and unfulfilling moments from his childhood in the bar that Christmas, Don moved toward my father. He told him he had something for him and he asked my father if he would go to the car with him to get it. My father agreed and the two of them headed out in the falling snow. Once they arrived, my brother grabbed a gift box from the car and handed it to him. It contained a flannel shirt.

My father opened it, and Don said, "I just want to know if you're ever gonna tell me you love me. I just want to know..." He sobbed as he waited, and when my father failed to reply, my brother pushed the issue. "You can't even say it once, can you?" To Don's total surprise, my father finally said it: "I love you." It was the first time he said it, and it was the last. He gave my brother a hug and walked away. Three months later, he took his own life.

At one point during my research, my mother shared again about some of her experiences with my dad. After recounting the incident when my father hit her and the police came, she suggested I go to the police department and request records of my father's arrests. With her incredible ability to detach from situations, my mother was rising above any drama and encouraging me to find the truth.

So I went to the police department and requested copies of all arrest records. There were four of them for his four arrests in a four-year, three-month span from August 9, 1978 to November 20, 1982. The last arrest occurred two months before he took his own life.

I don't know if it was the validation these reports provided about his sad life—again—or the continuing grief that my family had such a poor role model for a father and husband, but I was stunned by their starkness. The arrest records were just as black-and-white as the police report detailing his suicide, and I was once again startled to see my father's life framed in that sterile method. Given what I already knew about his history, the new information showed no surprises. It was unending active alcoholic behavior.

Report #1   August 9, 1978 (At his girlfriend's apartment. My father was 41 years old.)

> "At approx. 0105 hrs called... ref. a party getting into the apt through the rear window. At arrival spoke to [woman who lived in apartment, i.e., his girlfriend, and she] stated she paid the rent and showed two rent receipts in her name. She had been going with [Mr. Laplante] for a few years and wanted to end the relationship as [he] is always drunk... [His] eyes were red, bllood [sic] shot, and watery. He could hardly speak and needed the

railing on the porch for support... [He] stated he... had no where [sic] else to go. There was no doubt he was intoxicated and with no other options he was arrested for same."

Report #2 February 19, 1979 (At his girlfriend's apartment. My father was 41 years old.)

"[His girlfriend's daughter] found the above sitting inside and that he did not belong there. Upon entering the apartment found the front door to the apartment had been kicked in and a portion of it was lying on the floor. Upon entering the apartment found the above seated at the kitchen table and he was drinking a glass of beer... [His girlfriend] advised us LaPlante [sic] did not live there nor did she want him there... he refused to submit to arrest as he would not place his arms behind his back and struggled to get free... He was restrained and forcibly handcuffed."

Report #3 November 5, 1982 (At the scene of his car accident. My father was 45 years old. It was two-and-a-half months before he died by suicide.)

"Talked with witness... he stated that he observed a vehicle go up on sidewalk northerly, the driver seemed intoxicated hit wall in front... then went westerly... stopped, went into reverse and hit [car]... causing damage to left front of vehicle, large dent, and could not open left door... I then talked with Mr [sic] Laplante... I noticed a strong odor of alcoholic beverages on his breath... I advised Mr [sic] Laplante to get hold of his neighbor to make arrangements with him... advised him if he did not, he would go to Court... Received a call from [car owner] today he state [sic] that Mr Laplante has not contacted him yet."

This car accident was one of my father's financial obligations that could have been causing the stress mentioned in the suicide police report.

Report #4 November 20, 1982 (At a local club. My father was 45 years old. It was two months before he died by suicide. Police report was in all capitals.)

"[THE NIGHT MANAGER & CLUB PRESIDENT]... EXPLAINED TO ME THAT AT 2000 HRS. OFF ... HAD REMOVED [my father]... FROM THE CLUB AS HE WAS INTOXICATED AND HAD BEEN CAUSING A DISTURBANCE. I ASKED LAPLANTE AND HE SAID THAT HE HAD BEEN REMOVED EARLIER AND THAT HE AGREED NOT TO RETURN. BOTH [NIGHT MANAGER & CLUB PRESIDENT] WANTED LAPLANTE OUT AGAIN. I ADVISED LAPLANTE SEVERAL TIMES THAT HE WOULD HAVE TO LEAVE AND COME BACK WHEN HE WAS SOBER TO TALK WITH THE [PRESIDENT]. HE ADVISED ME THAT HE WAS NOT LEAVING UNTIL HE WAS DONE WITH [THE PRESIDENT]. I INFORMED HIM THAT THIS WAS HIS LAST WARNING TO

LEAVE AND COME BACK SOMEOTHER [sic] TIME AND AGAIN HE REFUSED SAYING HE WAS STAYING. AT THIS TIME I PALCED [sic] LAPLANTE UNDER ARREST… AND HAD HIM TRANSPORTED TO H.Q."

The arrests listed in reports three and four occurred two-and-a-half and two months, respectively, before my father's suicide in January 1983. The words of the reports made my body shudder. Even after hearing about the abusive behavior my mother was subject to, I had this vision that my father was a quiet drunk. I envisioned him in bars, sitting there drinking alone, but I didn't envision him hassling managers. I also didn't envision him treating his girlfriend the way he treated my mother. I had an unfounded and naïve vision that once my father went to live with his girlfriend, his romantic and family relationships were smooth and easy going. I thought he abandoned us because he liked them better.

Memorable Minutiae Nine

When I was in high school, my father had a job where he managed the storefront at one of the local billiard pool halls. That was where he taught my brothers and sisters and me how to play. I still play today on occasion. Some of my siblings do as well.

My father took a job with a beer delivery company one year. To no one's surprise, he was caught drinking on the job more than once. And more than once his workers' union sought recourse for him with management and got him reinstated. He didn't deserve to keep his job, but we were glad he could. Nonetheless, he went to bars and drank most of our money away. He was oblivious to family responsibility.

10

Memorials

One autumn day, I took another drive to visit my father at the mausoleum. I came across a notice inside the building that stated the management was offering the guardians of each crypt the opportunity to buy a poinsettia as part of a memorial display at Christmas. I felt moved to participate. I wrote down the information and called the mausoleum when I returned home. I thought it would be a good idea to ask my brothers and sisters to join in, so I contacted each of them and explained the situation. Two siblings went in on the gesture, and three declined. I didn't expect such a dichotomy. At most, I expected only one of my siblings to say no.

From California, my brother Greg said something like, "That man never did a thing for me. I have no desire to do something like that for him." His words reverberated through me, but I respected his ability to tap into and articulate his feelings so definitively. It was the first time I realized anyone had such a drastically different reaction from mine. I assumed he was angry and hurt, but I didn't ask. I wasn't comfortable talking with him about something that could become emotional for me. Given that so many years had passed, and Greg had several deaths in his life during that time, he could have learned how to internalize these occurrences and been matter-of-fact about the whole thing.

When the cemetery mailed me an invitation to participate in the poinsettia memorial the following year, I accepted, but I did it on my own. I was too skittish to ask everyone again. The third year, I declined and stopped contributing to the Christmas poinsettia memorial for my dad.

Five years later, I received a notice from Mount Calvary Cemetery and Mausoleum about an Easter lily memorial. I don't know why, but it was the first Easter notice I ever received. I asked myself, *"Should I participate on my own again, or should I contact my siblings and let them know about the memorial?"* At first, I thought I would do it on my own. I felt unprepared to deal with the potentially contentious responses. After careful thought, however, I decided I would simply find a way to deal with the upheavals, and I contacted all five of my siblings.

I was expecting the Great Divide again, but I was wrong. Instead of three and three, the split ended up at four and two, four wanting to participate and two not wanting to participate. Diane, who didn't contribute to the Christmas poinsettia years earlier, had a change of heart. She sent me a handwritten note that said, "I used to be angry and ashamed of Dad for a long time, but over the years, I've realized he was a victim of his vices and now I no longer harbor any anger toward him." My eyes filled with tears of joy. I was so happy for her. It was such a relief to know she no longer carried the burden of spite within her.

The two siblings who declined, simply said, "No thank you."

There have been other memorials in acknowledgment of my father. Lynn requested memorial Masses for him. Known as Requiem Masses, they are offered for the repose of the souls of the dead, so they might have peace and eternal rest. Don walked in Out of the Darkness walks for the American Foundation for Suicide Prevention (AFPS).

After I returned to the Catholic Church in 1997, I followed Lynn's lead. I requested memorial Masses for my father, and I continue to do so on his birthday and mine. I also remembered my father with the St. Gerard Walkathon I founded. This event consisted of a five-mile walk to raise money for girls and women facing unexpected pregnancies. In the Catholic Church, St. Gerard is the patron saint of expectant mothers; he is all about bringing new life into our world. Many baby boys have been named after him.

I didn't start the walkathon specifically with my father in mind, but I thought of him many times during my planning sessions.

Life   <> Death
Birth   <> Abortion
Living <> Committing suicide

The contrasts were disquieting. I remembered what I'd learned about my mother's crisis pregnancy. She and my father could have been mentors for the event. Their family life wasn't perfect, but they didn't discard any of their children via abortion. Otherwise, my sister Diane, in particular, might not be alive today.

We raised a total of $17,000 during the five times we held the St. Gerard Walkathon. The money was donated to two local nonprofit organizations, a Birthright office, where crisis pregnancy counseling and initial supplies are provided, and Spring House, a shelter for women facing crisis pregnancies. Providentially, I held the walk every year during the month of June, which is the month in which my father was born. The walkathon was gratifying. It was an effort that honored the dignity of human life, something my father gave up of his own free will. Nonetheless, he had me and probably several other family members praying for him.

In 2013, I received another invitation to participate in a Christmas poinsettia memorial for my father at Mount Calvary's mausoleum. Without hesitation, I called the telephone number on the form. When I double-checked with the attendant in charge about the schedule for the display, she asked me for my father's name and looked up his information on her computer. When she found it, she casually said, "Oh, he's in the Resurrection chapel," and I immediately asked, "When you say he is in the Resurrection chapel, do you mean that the whole mausoleum is called the Resurrection chapel?" "No," she said. "Your father is in the section that is called the Resurrection chapel. Other areas are named after the Blessed Mother, the American Saints, and the Sacred Heart."

Once again, this providential nature of my father's burial place provided me hope. Of all the different areas in the mausoleum, he landed in the Resurrection chapel. It's not that I expected my father would be definitively resurrected and saved simply because of the chapel where he was buried. There are no certainties with things like that. I do believe, though, that God allows what we might call "coincidences" to happen, in order to give us reason to continue hoping and praying that our loved ones will be reunited with Him.

Memorable Minutiae Ten

My father had his nickname, Blackie, tattooed on his upper right arm. Like him, I had and have dark skin. It comes from our particular lineage of French Canadian and Native American (Canadian), something of which we were both quite proud.

One time, my father came home and found his clothes in garbage bags on our front porch. My mother had kicked him out of our house—again. I don't know how many times it actually happened, but it plays back in my mind like the replay feature of a DVD player, until my mother throws him out one last time—and my father never comes back.

11

Intimacy

Intimacy wasn't something I knew growing up. I didn't know it as a vocabulary word or as an experience, even well into my adult life. It took me many years to recognize when I was experiencing it, and I was surprised that it was often with my two sons. When my older son, Kegan, was in grade school, he wrote a note one night and left it on my bed. It said, *"Dear Mom, I'm sorry what just happened but I was kind of jealous of Alden getting a POKE Ball and beetin grandpa If you want to find me look under the Bed Kegan."*

When my younger son, Alden, was in seventh grade, he had to write a paper for his health class. "Mom, I picked the topic of depression for my health class project. Can I interview you for it?" he asked. "I have to type up the answers and create a brochure and poster, and then I have to hand them all in next Wednesday." I was thrilled about his lack of inhibition about the topic, and without hesitation, I said yes.

He created his list of interview questions, and I typed my answers on the computer while he fell asleep that night. Back in school, Alden created his brochure.

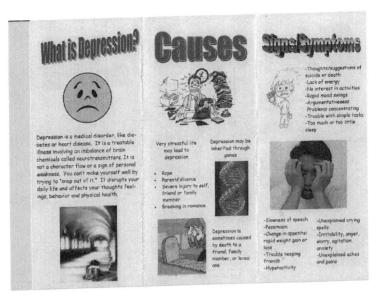

Alden's brochure about depression, created at age thirteen.

My sons have also shown me that intimacy can be as simple as a phone call. "Hi Mom, it's me Alden calling. Just checking in since I missed you on Sunday night when you called. I've been really busy with midterms. I'll try to call you back tomorrow because after that I'll be pretty busy into this coming weekend. I hope we can chat. I love you."

These types of messages always stir loving sentiments in my heart, sentiments I was unable to feel many years ago.

When the boys started college, we established a "Let's check in on Sundays" routine. I'm still in a bit of disbelief that we've continued with it for more than four years.

When text messaging was introduced several years ago, I resisted it at first. It felt abrupt and cold. After watching others use it for a while, I recognized it's like all other technology. It can be used for good and it can be used for bad. While using text messaging, Kegan and Alden and I have laughed, made up our own shorthand, shared sad moments, and relayed the mundane:

> ☙ "It went really well! Now we have a bunch of work to do, which is good :)"
> ☙ "Bummer that Memere can't make it. :(. Does noon work?"
> ☙ "xoxo"
> ☙ "Hey mom, sorry I haven't responded. Yes I will be able to talk tomorrow, I'm really sorry to hear about Francis :("
> ☙ "love and miss you too !"
> ☙ "HAPPY BIRTHDAY !!!!!!"
> ☙ "things are great ! thanks for thinkin of me :) "
> ☙ "Happy new year mom!"
> ☙ "Thanks mom :) Two more exams and work on Friday then I'm on break!"
> ☙ "Yep! On the bus to Boston right now, then headed up to dads :)"
> ☙ "Just saw that! Why do they rename the pope?"
> ☙ "I know, I wish we had been able to come closer to Christmas, and I'm really sorry I botched the Yankee swap. I think [we] will be coming on the ."
> ☙ "happy easter mum! back to san fran today, cant wait to see ya in a month!"

I save my sons' text messages until I absolutely have to delete them. I like to boost my spirits by rereading them while I wait to be called in for my appointment at a doctor's office. One year when Kegan and I had exchanged a lot of text messages, I had this whim to archive them in some kind of a Christmas present for him. I transcribed each one into a Word document I set up, and then I printed them out. I cut them into individual strips, folded them, put them all in a brown bag, and tied the bag with a ribbon. Then I placed it under our Christmas tree.

When it was time to open our gifts, I was a bit tentative about what Kegan's reaction would be to the brown paper bag. I handed it to him, he looked into it, and his face lit up as he pulled out the strips of paper and figured out what they were. He was thrilled. He sat on the floor, flattened each message, and read them one by one. He tried to guess what was happening in our lives when each of them transpired, and his guesses were amazingly accurate. On that wonderful morning, my gnawing insecurity was dispelled, one strip of paper at a time, as I realized I was an adequate mother after all.

The nature of intimacy is often revealed by the names people use to address one another. This played out with my father and Kegan and Alden. Whenever I mentioned him to them as they were growing up, I felt anxious. I didn't know what to call him. "Your grandfather" felt too personal, because they never experienced him in person. They should have; they should have had their grandfather, but he was dead before they were even born. Also, I was ashamed of my father.

With time, I settled on "my father." "Yes, your dark skin comes from my father." "My father was really smart in school. He skipped two grades." I kept that safety net up for them. "My father" instead of "your grandfather" put distance between them. It kept my sons removed from his suicide and from the shame and grief and embarrassment that accompanies it. They were also kept distant from his alcoholism, adultery, and abandonment, or so I convinced myself.

Alden once pointed out how I had gone one step further. Not only did I not call my father "your grandfather," I didn't call him Pépère, which is the more informal and intimate French Canadian address. It's not like they didn't know about his suicide or illnesses. I introduced the topics to them when they were quite young. I talked about them much earlier than my brothers and sisters talked with their children, because I was adamant that that family history wasn't going to fester as a secret. I also wanted them to have the information so they could tailor their lifestyles if necessary.

Memorable Minutiae Eleven

Aunt Nancy wrote to me once and said my dad could have made something of himself. Like her, he was self-taught. He studied psychology for a season. He had lots of books and read and read. He couldn't seem to soak up enough about a subject in which he had an interest. She looked up to him for that.

One summer morning, my father's brother, Édouard, drove him to visit my elderly grandmother at Aunt Nancy's house. My father was drunk. He had a can of beer in one pocket and a bottle of wine in his hand. He gave the wine to my grandmother, who, along with my aunt, was quite displeased. When it was time for them to leave, Aunt Nancy said sarcastically, "Gee Blackie, I hope you come back to visit Mom next summer." She rolled her eyes. My grandmother followed up by saying, "Oh, who knows if I'll even be here next year?" to which my father replied, "Don't worry, Mom, I'll be gone before you." And he was. He took his life less than six months after that.

12

Turning Fifty

I was cleaning my house one day when there was a knock at the door. "Who is it?" I asked. "It's us," answered Diane and Patty, the two sisters who had come to my college apartment twenty-nine years earlier to tell me my father had committed suicide. This time, though, my mother, Kegan, and Alden were with them. When I opened the door, they were standing there holding balloons and streamers and shouting, "Happy Birthday!"

It was a surprise visit to celebrate my fiftieth birthday. Unlike my birthday in 1983, I was clearheaded. Blackouts were a thing of the past. My mind was lucid and my heart was warm as I watched my family hang decorations on my living room wall. We were all excited to be together, especially for my milestone birthday. We mingled for a while, and then went out for a jazz brunch, their treat. Once we were settled at our table, the staff brought over a big balloon and tied it to my chair. They also sang "Happy Birthday" and gave me a special dessert later on. I enjoyed the attention and wasn't at all embarrassed by the hubbub around me.

When we finished at the restaurant, my sons and I returned home and my mother and sisters returned to theirs. We hadn't talked at all about my father's death, and I was glad. I needed a little limelight for myself that day.

Still, he was never far from my thoughts. At one point, I found myself saying some private prayers for him. The *Memorare* was my favorite. It is a petition to Mary, the mother of Jesus. I asked her to intercede on behalf of my father, for forgiveness and mercy from God.

> *"Remember O most gracious Mary, that never was it known that anyone who fled to thy protection, implored thy help or sought thy intercession, was left unaided. Inspired with this confidence, I fly unto thee, O Mother of the Word Incarnate. Despise not my petitions but in thy mercy hear and answer them. Amen."*

Later, I remembered the Requiem Mass I requested for him at a local monastery. Gratitude and hope washed over me as I envisioned the monks offering prayers for his soul during their daily Mass that morning.

Memorable Minutiae Twelve

In the early stages of their marriage, my mother and father double-dated with my mother's sister and her boyfriend. My aunt told me they had some wonderful times together when my father was sober. She still has fond memories of him being a lot of fun back then.

That same aunt used to babysit us on Friday nights. After she put us all to bed, she slept over in our living room. When my mom and dad came home, my father was usually drunk and yelling at my mother. My aunt would put a pillow over her head to drown out the noise and squelch her fear. She was afraid of my father when he was in that state.

13

Silver Linings

Like people who comb the beach with a metal detector after a storm, I combed my life with psychotherapy and Catholicism after my father's suicide. Instead of finding coins and other metal valuables, I found insights and spiritual gifts. Instead of finding litter and lost belongings, I uncovered self-defeating behaviors and aspects of my soul that were lost when I was a child.

At some point when I was trying to make sense of my circumstances and the pain present in them, I wished I had no father at all. *"That would certainly eliminate the abject and repulsive memories I have of him,"* I thought. But then I realized it would also eliminate the few heartwarming memories I had. In the end, I decided I didn't want that. I wanted to remember the good and the bad, accepting him as he was. It was a more realistic vantage point for me, and I had worked too hard to want anything else.

Depression made me think things could never get better. And that was essentially true, as long as my doctors and I couldn't find medications that worked, my support network remained stagnant, and I remained socially inactive. When it became severe enough, it was oppressive and debilitating. I remember waiting to put my boys down to sleep for the night so I could go to my bedroom, fall on my bed, and lay in the dark with my arm over my eyes, frozen in time. It was the only part of day when I completely gave into depression. My mind would either go blank or step into the black hole of desperation and not come out for what seemed like eons. I literally couldn't move.

My body felt like it weighed three times my actual weight, but when my husband walked in, I managed to lift it and go to my closet to pick out clothes for the next day. I didn't want him to know how bad it was. I would often stand in front of the closet, not knowing how much time had passed. My husband would eventually come over and I would snap out of my stupor. I wasn't going to let depression run my life.

Thankfully, God gifted me with the virtue of perseverance. I kept up with my therapy appointments, medication checks, all the chores needed for my children, time with my husband, and work, white-knuckling it all the way. When my sons were young and I didn't have it in me to change another diaper, I managed to find a way to change the next one, and several after that. When I thought I couldn't interview one more new therapist, I hung in there, made the next appointment, and completed the next interview. When Greg told me he didn't want anything to do with our father, I found a reservoir of grit and patience and eventually witnessed a change of heart toward him. And when I was sick from making phone calls to my health insurance company, instead of giving up, I overrode my malaise and made more calls until I finally connected with the person in charge of my account.

One might think it's no wonder that I didn't die by suicide long before I made my attempt. I think, though, I was afraid of that prospect as much as I was afraid of becoming more suffocated by my waking life. It was like standing at a window on the forty-fifth floor of a skyscraper in a blazing inferno, stuck between two horrific choices: suicide by jumping to my death or staying on the window ledge and dying by fire and asphyxia. But God's graceful gift of perseverance gave me just enough strength to hold my own. I say that as if I did it all, as if I made it all happen, but I know I didn't. When I finally got down on my knees and asked God to release the anger I was harboring toward people in my life, especially my former husband, and I did it again and again, things gradually improved. Jesus was able to play His important role as redeemer.

I eventually learned about uniting my sufferings to Christ's sufferings on the cross. At first it seemed like some sort of unhealthy denial of my human pain. It's not. It's the opposite. It's embracing the pain and joining it with Christ's pain to add to the spiritual well being of others—and therein lies the joy.

Of course, nothing in my life was as dramatic as what happened to Jesus, but uniting even the most minor of my sufferings to His proved to be uplifting. Any opportunity to participate with Him in bringing forgiveness and salvation to mankind, sometimes all of it, could be nothing less than uplifting.

This spiritual outlook and practice became an underpinning of my existence, and it continues to sustain me through dark days and joyous days. In fact, it sustains me through all days, because in the end, Jesus is the ultimate of silver linings. Through Him, I have stayed alive for my two sons, and through Him, I have passed my joy on to them, thereby becoming an instrument for the transformation of my family's legacy of despair to a legacy of hope.

Compared to me, my sons are better able to balance the ever-changing demands of friendships, work, leisure, romance, relationships with me and their father, investing for the future, and working out, among other things. With a family history like mine, though, it would be imprudent to say they're all set for the rest of their lives. I pray that they are, but if not, I hope the information and love around them will help them manage more readily than I can.

As I progressed through my "rite of passage," my perspective on life changed. I once found myself deeply moved when I chanced upon a friend's daughter arguing with her father.

"I just don't understand why you won't let me wear this shirt tonight," she retorted. "There is nothing wrong with it."

"You are twelve years old. I don't expect you to understand everything, but we have talked about this before," countered her dad. "That shirt is too low cut. Boys will be staring at your chest instead of making eye contact with you. Is that how you want to become friends with them?"

Most people would have been either distraught or unmoved by the exchange. I was initially distraught and then overcome with warmth and reassurance. Their argument was a sign of connection, of life and love, of stability and hope. They were engaging with and caring about each other, something I never had the opportunity to experience with my father.

I witnessed similar experiences between my sons and their father. They bantered about football statistics, disagreed about the time limit for playing video games, and didn't see eye-to-eye about who should shovel the recently fallen snow. Ultimately, they hung in there with each other.

I am grateful for having been privy to all of these interchanges because I discovered something new about love. Since my friend's daughter and my sons never had to experience the angst that comes from not knowing if your father will ever come home again, I felt a chasm between my world and theirs. I became convinced that they were unaware of how blessed they truly are to have loving fathers in their lives. That led me to wish that all these children could experience the gratitude I achieved after recovering from a dysfunctional family life. With time, however, I realized that identical life experiences aren't necessary for learning what true love is. The everyday, nontraumatic unfolding of life is sufficient for this lesson. My path was overkill.

After dealing with my father's alcoholism on her own for many years, my mother's world opened up when she attended Al-Anon, a twelve-step program for families and friends of alcoholics. Participants give and get support from each other by attending meetings on a regular basis and learning how to change their behavior toward the alcoholic. The changes also help the person create healthier relationships with children, neighbors, and coworkers.

Through Al-Anon, my mother realized she could create a safer, more serene life for my brothers, my sisters, and me. The people in it didn't tell her how to do that, but as she attended meetings and worked the program, she figured out the answers for her situation. With much angst, she finally kicked my father out of the house for good. She was a brave soul to do that, since she was a single mother of six without a high school diploma. She didn't know how she was going to support us all, but she knew that primary importance was safety.

Once all six of us children were in school, my mother found minimum-wage jobs at local fast-food restaurants, where she enjoyed being with other adults and contributing monetarily to the family. She didn't earn much, but she worked hard to make ends meet. Unfortunately, even with significant help from her parents, she couldn't accomplish that goal and had to face the reality that she needed public assistance.

My mother never expected to be in such a position. She never *wanted* to be in such a position. She was ashamed about it, but she went through the application processes for several public assistance programs. She wasn't going to turn away legitimate help. She secured food stamps, the free lunch program, welfare, government-subsidized dental and medical care, and subsidized housing. She managed to provide for us by being prudent with all her resources.

Unlike the fickle, naïve pride I had for my father, the pride I had for my mother lasted into my adult years. I will always be proud of her and grateful to her for enduring the personal humiliation inherent in getting public assistance. I will also be grateful and indebted to the greater community that funded the programs. We really needed them and benefited tremendously.

My mother was a hero. She persevered to provide for all of us, and she eventually worked her way off public assistance. In that sense, she was a role model for everyone receiving welfare, and she certainly deserved the retirement she had for several years before her death.

I have been fortunate to grow in my understanding and practice of prayer, which is a lifeline to God. Whether it's a Hail Mary, a "thank you" to God, a self-righteous complaint to Jesus, a call to the Holy Spirit for the right words in a conversation, or a plea for the salvation of my parents' souls, I know He is pleased to hear from me. Of course, He's probably not thrilled when I complain self-righteously, but I know He prefers that to my silence. So I do my best to stay connected.

I even stay connected in my most confusing and painful times. I tell Him everything: "Why are You keeping me alive? I never would have guessed that hell exists here on earth. This has to be it because I can't imagine anything worse. Please, please don't let me wake up tomorrow. It's pure agony, and I don't want the ceaseless screaming streaming through my body any more. Just take me."

I have ranted and pleaded with God in this way during many of my darkest hours. I believe He was listening to all of it and providing me comfort and help in ways I may not have even known.

In addition to my personal prayer, I have been blessed to have been taught the Rosary, which I pray every day. I hold the prayer beads to track where I am in the lengthy series of Hail Mary's, Our Father's, and Glory Be's, and I connect with the Holy Family, the Holy Trinity, and all the saints. In that way, my spiritual network and safety net is broadened.

The practice is meditative and brings me solace and reprieve from the material world. That isn't to say I never become depressed or that I find a quick way out through prayer. No. Our minds and bodies are imperfect, so prayer is not an end-all. It is, however, another powerful tool for staying alive and living in joy.

I have had many holy moments while praying the Rosary. Once, I received an internal knowing about the mystery called *Finding Jesus in the Temple.* I was meditating on Mary and Joseph finding Jesus after He was lost for three days. I realized all of us can experience the joy of finding Him, because we can literally find Him every day in the temple, or in our case, church or chapel. He is truly present, Body, Blood, Soul, and Divinity, in the Eucharist in all the tabernacles of our churches everywhere in the world. And He wants us to find Him there.

Another time, I was focusing on the mystery called *The Visitation.* Mary was three months pregnant with Jesus, and her cousin Elizabeth was six months pregnant with John the Baptist. Mary travelled by foot to offer Elizabeth help. This mystery showed me that we can pray to Mary any time and ask her to bring Jesus spiritually to us in our times of need.

Prayer can only evolve in faith, which is one reason I believe many psychiatrists and therapists don't know how to incorporate it into their practice. Psychology is considered a science, and many of them believe that religion doesn't mingle with science. I've found the opposite to be true. The most effective psychotherapy has transpired when my therapist has been skilled in at least embracing the spiritual aspect of healing. He didn't have to give lessons or lectures on how to pray, but when he showed how prayer and spirituality were useful in my repertoire in therapy, and encouraged me with it, great strides were made. I can only imagine how many clients have been undertreated due to this ignorance or resistance to learning.

There is another step beyond prayers, particularly on the communal level. It is going out and doing something for others, which is a physical manifestation of prayer. I have done a tremendous amount of this type of service in my community, as well as on a mission trip to the Appalachians. I did much of it while I was very depressed, and it often alleviated symptoms, at least for the rest of the day.

This played out prominently at the local food pantry, where I was trained to work the front desk. Registering those in need of food each week exposed me to the surprising prevalence of hunger in my small-town community. I was often reminded of my father on the day of his suicide, when he had no food in his refrigerator. It made me more grateful for what I had, and it helped me grow in compassion for others. Ironically, I needed that same compassion when I had to apply for assistance at the food pantry later. I had to leave the corporate world of engineering and take a 67 percent drop in income. The codirector of the food pantry encouraged me to apply for their services.

I hesitated until I remembered my mother going through similar procedures for food stamps and welfare. Recollections of her persistence in the face of shame helped me to overcome my own. I submitted an application. As always, the volunteer staff was welcoming with warm smiles and friendly conversation. The fact that they maintained a clean storefront and looked for ways to provide healthier foods, like whole grain breads and local produce, made it easier for me to go through with it. Working at the front desk became a way of giving back to an organization that exemplified the love of Jesus. The swap wasn't necessary, but it made me feel more at ease while accepting the help I needed.

I have since volunteered at the senior center, other walkathons, and the public library. My work there and the interactions with other employees helped fill some of the emptiness that accompanies depression and suicidal thinking. I have always been grateful for them as reenergizing outlets.

I don't imagine my father ever knew faith or hope. As far as I can tell, he never provided service to others, and he never sought spiritual or medical treatment. His most frequent justification for staying away from help was rooted in his complaints about the people involved.

He claimed that Alcoholics Anonymous (AA) members were hypocrites because they would get drunk after their twelve-step meetings. I learned that wasn't true when I attended AA in an effort to learn more about him. The truth was also attested to at twelve-step Al-Anon meetings for adult children of alcoholics. A small number of members might go drinking after meetings, but the majority of members stuck to the program. The wonderful thing about AA and the people in it is that they would have been straightforward with my father and told him he had a bad attitude—but then they would have encouraged him with one of the many slogans used in the program. In this case, "Keep coming back, it works if you work it" would have been a likely candidate.

Of course, recovery programs aren't perfect, but I didn't see that as cause enough to give up on them. In some ways defects can make a program more effective. They provide an opportunity, in a safe environment, to learn how to contend with imperfections and the hiccoughs of life. These are things my father never learned how to do. Why do some people get it and some people don't?

When my brothers and sisters and I had children, we finally found the voice that was long absent throughout the generations of our family. I can't recall ever hearing my parents say, "I love you" to us or to each other. I can't recall ever hearing my grandparents say it to my mother or father either. As a result, we never said it to them or to each other. When we had our own children, though, we broke that cycle. We began telling our children "I love you," even before they could understand it.

Now, across generations, one can hear us saying it as we hang up the phone, send an e-mail, or hug to say goodbye at the end of a family gathering. We are all far from perfect, but those three words have become incontrovertible signs of progress and success. Counselors have confirmed that. They have told some of my brothers and sisters that given our father's alcoholism and abuse, his depression, our parents' divorce, our poverty, and our father hanging himself, we are lucky to have survived. They even postulated that perhaps by God's generous grace, and maybe even by a miracle, we were spared the dark chasm of suicide or other horrific death. It was the first time I heard therapists blending science and religion.

With lots of assistance from the community and medical providers, my brothers and sisters and I have been fortunate to beat the odds. We have established fulfilling lives for our children and ourselves, and in doing so, we have ingrained in our families and future generations what is probably the most powerful deterrent to suicide: love.

Memorable Minutiae Thirteen

I can't recall more than twelve positive memories about my father. Twelve isn't very many, even for a fractured existence with a parent, but I am grateful I have them.

My brother Don said he doesn't have any positive memories of our dad.

Epilogue

I am not naïve. I know depression. I know its haunting nature and its gripping hold. This week. Next year. One significant upset and it can return, even after long periods of reprieve. It can make me think I want to commit suicide again, as it did while I was writing this book. It's like most cancers. A person might survive one or many episodes, but he or she will live with the anxiety of wondering if and/or when it's going to come back.

At the same time, there are positive aspects of depression. It has brought me an emotional sensitivity that I didn't have before, such that my ability to feel compassion for others and myself has deepened. I have also gained the gift of patience and a more artistic and romantic outlook on life.

Perhaps a more accurate way of describing the positive aspects of depression is to call them fruits of the struggle to survive. Of all the fruits, medication and prayer were the most vital for me. Until I had them in place, my healing did not take root.

Healing and all, when I neared the completion of this book, fear gripped me. *"What if I end up committing suicide? What if, in the end, I fail? Maybe I shouldn't publish this book after all. If I end up killing myself, my sons will have to face a greater shame than I did."* The thoughts ran on. *"What if suicide and depression ultimately win?"* I felt like an underdog, and I pined for the safety of my sons.

I managed the situation by going back to basics: prayer, faith, therapy, medication, friends, and family. They are the source of my inner calm. They make up the only approach I know that substantially increases my chances of having a suicide-free life. They can bring joy amid suffering, and they can weaken the stronghold of suicide clustering on future generations.

* * *

My mother read my manuscript before she unexpectedly passed away. She also made herself graciously available for questions I had, and I had some painful ones. At some point during our exchanges, she turned seventy-five. My brothers and sisters and I threw her a surprise birthday party. Our aunts, uncles, her neighbors, cousins, grandchildren, godchildren, in-laws, and former bosses all came to celebrate her life. It was a beautiful testimonial.

When we sorted through her belongings a few months later, Patty found my manuscript on her kitchen table. Seeing it there brought everything together for me. In that moment, I understood my mother had loved as Jesus had loved, even if she never made the connection. For all the horrible things my father did, she never denigrated the essence of his being. She recounted his poor behavior accurately, but she never demeaned him. It was as if she intuitively knew that my father, a blatant sinner, was made in the image of God, and therefore deserved to be recognized as such.

Photographs

My father catching a fish at five years old, 1942.

My father, age 7

My grandfather, age 44,
one year before his death.

My father's family, 1944.

My First Communion, 1969.
St. Jean de Baptiste Church.

My father with his seven siblings.
He is fourth from the left in the back row.

My mother when I
was in high school.

Me in high school,
1979.

My siblings and I at the Rock Rimmon Federal Housing Project, 1969.

Family gathering, 2009.

My sons and I at Alden's college graduation, 2014.

Me at a gymnastics
meet, 1978.

My father and Uncle Jerry
at Sandy Beach, 1968.

Easter Sunday, 1968.
I am on the far right
of the front row.

My mother with the first five of us children
in California, 1962. My younger brother is
not yet born. I am on her lap.

Appendices

Throughout the years, I have used writing to make sense of my confusion, sadness, and healing. I originally wrote in private journals, but over time, I authored articles for publication. Four of the articles are included here in hope that readers will be enlightened in some additional way by at least one of them.

Appendix I

Suicide Runs In Families

My Dad tried it. I tried it. He used a belt. I used pills. He physically cut off oxygen to his brain. I chemically cut it off. He succeeded and died. I failed and lived.

He was 45 years old when he completed suicide. I was in my 30's when I tried. He was depressed. So was I. He was alone in his apartment. So was I. He didn't come back. I did. I woke up and went to the hospital, where I recounted my story. My days and dates didn't match those of the staff. We eventually figured out that I was passed out for two days before I came to. No one knew I was there.

Our outsides didn't match our insides. My father and I were both smart. One time in school, he advanced a grade. And then he did it again another year. I was salutatorian of my high school class. They voted me Most Intelligent and Most Likely to Succeed. I was first in my college chemical engineering class, Summa Cum Laude, and often first in my groups in the corporate work world.

My Dad was acrobatic and did diving and stunts. I was a gymnast. He had six wonderful children. I had two. Suicide is real. I could give you statistics, but I won't. Real people, real problems. One of my cousins also tried suicide. Like my father, he succeeded. Real people, real problems.

If anyone tells you they don't want to live or they tell you they have a plan, take them seriously. They are indirectly crying for help, something neither my father nor I did at the time. Call a suicide help line, or call 911 if you have to. Get help.

And please remember—people considering Euthanasia and Assisted Suicide need help to. They are no more in their "right minds" than people doing it on their own. They are all missing God in their lives, as well as the truth about the power of suffering when it is united to Christ on the Cross. How many souls can be saved!

I'm guessing many people did a lot of redemptive suffering to save my soul. Thanks to them, the predictions of my high school class have come true. I am indeed intelligent, and now I am quite successful – at least from God's point of view. Peace.

Source: TASTE AND SEE [http://www.tasteandsee2.blogspot.com], June 10, 2010.

Appendix II

July 2, 2010

Wandering In The Desert

I am walking in the desert, not knowing what God wants of me right now. Or maybe it's that I know and I don't like it. After all, who likes hanging out in the desert, parched, feeling like *"Be still and know that I am God"* is the hardest thing in the world to live out?

I am grateful to God, though, that I tuck away papers with prayers on them everywhere in my house, often forgetting them and finding them in times like this. I just found the one below as I was doing some much needed cleaning in my office. It was on my bulletin board in a hanger I made with popsicle sticks about fifteen years ago. It's fitting for today.

> *"I have no idea where I am going. I do not see the road ahead of me. I cannot know for certain where it will end. Nor do I really know myself, and the fact that I think that I am following your will does not mean that I am actually doing so. But I believe that the desire to please You does, in fact, please You. And I hope I have that desire in all that I am doing. I hope that I will never do anything apart from that desire. And I know that if I do this You will lead me by the right road though I may know nothing about it. Therefore will I trust You always though I may seem to be lost and in the shadow of death. I will not fear, for You are ever with me, and You will never leave me to face my perils alone."*

— Thomas Merton

Source: TASTE AND SEE [http://www.tasteandsee2.blogspot.com/2010/07/wandering-in-desert.html]

Appendix III

November 14, 2011

American Foundation for Suicide Prevention

Kudos to my brother who did his second *Out of the Darkness* walk this year. It is put on by the *American Foundation for Suicide Prevention (AFSP)*, whose goal is to understand and prevent suicide through research, education and advocacy. The walks are held across the country.

My brother walked as a tribute to my father, who committed suicide back in 1983. I was 21 and he was 24, but we were much younger than that when my father struggled with alcoholism. We talked about the impact our father's suicide had on us, and still has on us. We just exchanged a few sentences, but the exchange was incredibly profound. How nice that we can talk about it now.

For me, many years later, thoughts will appear out of the blue, about how much I missed out on due to his absence. **I would not wish suicide on any family.**

Thank you, Don, for raising awareness with your walks. It is such a ProLife thing that you do.

Source: TASTE AND SEE [http://www.tasteandsee2.blogspot.com /2011/11/kudos-to-my-brother-who-did-his-second.html]

Appendix IV

Thank God I Made It Home

By Kathleen Laplante

The story of my religious conversion.

I remember it clearly. My husband and I decided to leave the Church, and we invited his Catholic parents over to justify ourselves. It was 1990 and we recently had our first son. With him on my hip, I stood in front of my mother-in-law and addressed the topic of abortion. Acerbic and ignorant, I asked, "Who does the Catholic Church think they are, telling me I can't have an abortion if I want one?" *"Sacred Heart of Jesus, have mercy on me."*

My in-laws were terror-stricken. They tried to explain the Faith and thought we should talk to a priest, but our minds were made up. The Devil had won. How else could I have held the life from my own womb, and argue that I should be able to abort "it" if I wanted to? And why else would I have been glad that my son would not have to bear the burdens of being female? (I did not know the dignity and joy of being a woman.)

The dichotomy of that scene alarms me now, but from our misinformed view of the world, our thinking could not have been different. We were enslaved by the insidious messages of the secular world. We hit all the hot-button topics of our generation, fulminating that "Women should be allowed to be priests. Gay couples should be able to live together and raise children. Confession is unnecessary. The idea that the Pope 'is king,' is archaic and ridiculous, and by the way, "Who is he to say we can't have premarital sex or use birth control?" *"Oh, God, forgive us our trespasses."*

My in-laws were disheartened to see us leave the Catholic Church for a Protestant one, but we were in "heaven." This Protestant congregation allowed women to preach, gay couples to live together, and anyone to receive "communion" any time, i.e. there was no confession. They did not (overtly) oppose abortion, and they were more hospitable. Our vagrant souls could not have wanted anything more – until that routine became too inconvenient and we stopped going to church again.

After my second son, I had an unexpected revolt against contraception. I knew something was wrong. Perhaps my pregnancies and births awakened the womanhood within me. My husband wanted a vasectomy, but I would not agree. Nor would I agree to go back on the pill. The strain in our relationship loomed with oppression. Simultaneously, my struggle with postpartum depression lingered on into major depression.

With serious illness at our relatively young age, disagreement about our sex life, and no conjugal faith to draw upon, our nine-year marriage ended in divorce. I was resentful about being a mother who lacked emotional stamina and know-how for fulfilling that role. I was also limited in my caretaking abilities due to my depression. So we agreed our sons should live with their father.

I was deeply torn about being the non-custodial parent. How could *I*, the mother, "give my children away?" Logically, I could, because they were going to their father, who loved them deeply and could take care of them better than I could. Emotionally however, I could not come to terms with it. Like my own father, I eventually felt that life was not worth living.

I ruminated about suicide many times. I made different plans. I even acted on one of them. Contrary to my father though, I overcame that ultimate act of escapism. I finally took God's hand, and when I did, He poured graces upon me. Along with leading me to outstanding medical help, he led me back to the Catholic Church. My life has never been the same. *"Come Holy Spirit; renew the face of the earth."*

Ironically, my Unitarian friend was God's first catalyst in my return. Seeing how distraught I was after my divorce, she suggested I regroup at the Guest House of a local Abbey. I had no idea what an Abbey was, but I did know this one had affordable rates in a serene location.

While I was there, the few-but-oh-so-precious seeds, planted during my barren Catholic upbringing, came out of dormancy. They began to grow when I realized I was on Catholic ground. I had a sudden panic to get information on annulments. For the first time, I realized my part in my marriage was not right in the eyes of God. Somehow I knew the annulment process was the key to my healing.

I asked one of the priests about it. That led to in-depth catechesis where we unraveled the ignorance, sinfulness, and confusion I had about contraception, freedom to marry, abortion, the value and dignity of life, motherhood, the dignity of being a woman, and more. I experienced a tremendous release of guilt, shame and confusion — I was coming home.

On October 7, 1997, the Feast of Our Lady of the Most Holy Rosary, I was formally received back into the Catholic Church. It was the foundation of my conversion, but not the end of it. The seeds of faith from my childhood continued to grow as I was catechized, spiritually directed, and guided in the practice of the Faith.

I no longer support the use of contraception – and now I know why. I no longer approve of abortion, and my sons clearly know my views on premarital sex and practicing purity in preparation for marriage. I defend the Church's teaching about the priesthood being reserved for men only. (My Unitarian friend even came to see the light on that topic.) The act of gay couples living together and raising families is no longer acceptable in my eyes.

I have been blessed to have my irreverent attitudes removed. I no longer say "I can connect with God any time, so I don't have to go to Mass." Instead, I draw upon the advice of my spiritual director — "Don't say 'I have to go to Mass;' say 'I get to go to Mass.'" And that I do. I now go to Sunday and daily Mass.

With a love for unborn babies and their mothers, I founded and coordinated an annual walkathon for expectant mothers in need of support for giving birth to their children. We held five walks and reached a grand total mark of $17,000 for a local counseling center and shelter. My relationships with my family, friends, and God, are strong. The Rosary is one of the most important tools I have, and I pray it almost every day. I am a Benedictine Oblate at the Abbey where it all began. I no longer work in the corporate world where I found it difficult to [get support] to act morally. I bake at the Abbey and I do some writing and editing.

I no longer see depression as a sign of failure. Instead, I view it as a manageable medical condition that has redemptive value when I unite it to Christ on the Cross. The Memorial Bible my family received when my Dad completed suicide on my birthday in 1983, has become another important and Providential resource. The process to obtain a Decree of Nullity brought the healing and growth I anticipated. The Magisterium's wisdom shined through in that area. My sons and I are emotionally close, and I love being their mother.

I am a Roman Catholic woman with no desire to be anything else. Christ replaced my hopelessness and disconnects with His joy and spiritual integration. The life I literally thought was hell, has become a foretaste of heaven. *"Thanks be to God. He brought me home."*

Source: CatholicMatch.com

Notes

1. Harvard Health Publications: Harvard Medical School, *Left Behind After Suicide*, July 2009, http://www.health.harvard.edu/newsletters/Harvard_ Womens_Health_Watch/2009/July/Left-behind-after-suicide

2. Harvard Mental Health Letter, Psychotherapists and patients confront the high cost of "low-grade" depression. *Dysthymia, Harvard Mental Health Letter*, February 2005.

3. Natural News: Natural Health News and Scientific Discoveries, *Experts say antidepressant drugs cause suicides instead of preventing them*, April 2006, http://www.naturalnews.com/019342_antidepressants_big_ pharma.html Also, see Pristiq: EXTENDED RELEASE TABLETS, *Does Depression Hold You Back From What You Enjoy?* 2013, https://www. pristiq.com/index.aspx

4. *Catechism of the Catholic Church*, New York: Doubleday, p. 550, 1994.

5. Ibid.

6. New American Bible, Nashville: Memorial Bibles International, Inc., 1976.

7. Psychiatric Times, *The Relationship of Suicide Risk to Family History of Suicide and Psychiatric Disorders*, December 2003, http://www. psychiatrictimes.com/articles/ relationship-suicide-risk-family-history-suicide-and-psychiatric-disorders

8. Safety Planning Intervention: A brief intervention for reducing suicide risk, About safety planning, 2014, http://www.suicidesafetyplan.com/ About_Safety_Planning.html

9. Stone, Geo, *Suicide and Attempted Suicide: Methods and Consequences*. New York: Caroll & Graf Publishers, A Division of Avalon Publishing Group, p. 344-346, p. 352, 1999.

Resources

BOOKS

Alcoholics Anonymous: The Big Book, 4th Edition. New York: Alcoholics Anonymous World Services, Inc., 2001.

Catechism of the Catholic Church. New York: Doubleday, 1994.

Confraternity of Christian Doctrine (author), United States Conference of Catholic Bishops (editor), *New American Bible Revised Edition*, Charlotte, NC: Saint Benedict Press, 2011.

Culling, Katy Sara. *Dark Clouds Gather: The True Story about Surviving Mood Disorders, Eating Disorders, Attempted Suicide and Self-Harm.* Essex, UK: Chipmunkapublishing Ltd., 2008.

Jamison, Kay Redfield. *Night Falls Fast: Understanding Suicide.* New York: Vintage Books, 1999.

Rappaport, Nancy. *In Her Wake: A Child Psychiatrist Explores the Mystery of Her Mother's Suicide.* New York: Basic Books, 2009.

The Vatican. *The Catechism of the Catholic Church Popular and Definitive Edition*, New York: Bloomsbury Academic, 2000.

Ugarte, Francisco. *From Resentment to Forgiveness: A Gateway to Happiness*, New York: Scepter Publishers, Inc., 2008.

Wickersham, Joan. *The Suicide Index: Putting My Father's Death in Order.* San Diego: Harcourt, Inc., 2008.

WEBSITES

American Foundation for Suicide Prevention http://www.afsp.org/

Alcoholics Anonymous http://www.aa.org/

Depression Chat Rooms http://www.depression-chat-rooms.org/

National Institute of Mental Health Depression http://www.nimh.nih.gov/health/topics/depression/index.shtml

Recognizing the Warning Signs of Suicide http://www.webmd.com/depression/guide/depression-recognizing-signs-of- suicide

See A New Sun Foundation http://www.4sans.org

Suicide Attempt Survivors http://www.suicidology.org/web/guest/
suicide-attempt-survivors

Suicide Prevention, Awareness and Support http://www.suicide.org/
Teen Suicide Prevention: Hope and Healing for Depression http://www.
ucantberased.com/

Thinking About Suicide? http://www.suicidology.org/web/guest/thinking-
about-suicide
Why does God let us suffer? https://www.youtube.com/
watch?v=gJUJpWI4xDk

With Help Comes Hope, support for persons living with suicidal thoughts
and suicide attempts http://lifelineforattemptsurvivors.org/

8 Helpful Websites for Coping with Depression http://www.health.com/
health/gallery/0,,20521915,00.html

12 Great Blogs for People with Depression http://www.health.com/health/
gallery/0,,20418363,00.html

Acknowledgments

I wish to thank Lois Cooperstein Linsky for encouraging me early on to expand my two-page story into a book. I also wish to thank everyone in my family and extended family who journeyed into the recesses of their minds and hearts to review my manuscripts. For those who declined to participate, I thank them as well for their authenticity.

I would like to recognize my editor, Stephen Parolini; my copyeditor, Lora Schrock; my cover designer, Samantha Malinay; my interior designer and typesetter, Pat Reinheimer; my psychiatrist, Robert M. Stern, M.D.; my spiritual counselor, Fr. Marc Crilly O.S.B.; and a consultant, Fr. Michael McEwen. Their interest, support, and confidence were instrumental in my bringing everything together.

Lastly, I want to thank and pay tribute to my two sons, Kegan and Alden, for reading and providing feedback on my manuscripts and cover designs. Given the nature of the topic, their generosity is commendable. It has been a joy to spend time with them during this treasured interchange.

About the Author

KATHLEEN LAPLANTE was born and raised in Manchester, New Hampshire. She obtained a bachelor of science from the University of New Hampshire and worked for several years as a chemical engineer. She is now a writer, an editor, and a baker. Kathleen lives outside of Boston and is the mother of two distinguished young men.

Made in the USA
Middletown, DE
09 June 2015